WEIGHING EVIDENCE

DISCOVER HOW THE EVIDENCE FROM
SCIENCE, ARCHAEOLOGY & PROPHECY
CONFIRMS THE ACCURACY OF THE BIBLE

BY

Dr E.K. VICTOR PEARCE
B.Sc.,Dip.Anth.,(Oxon) M.R.E.,D.Ed.,F.R.A.I.,C.F.

Raans Road, Amersham-on-the-Hill, Bucks, HP6 6JQ

Text abridged from Evidence For Truth:
Science, Archaeology and Prophecy
Edited by **Claire Meikle**
and Sub-edited by **Juliet Taylor**

ISBN 1 872059 91 0

British Library Catalogue-in-Publication Data
A catalogue record for this book is available
from the British Library.

Cover photographs:
Telegraph Colour Library

Disclaimer: Every effort has been made to obtain the necessary permissions to
reproduce the illustrations in this book, however the publishers apologise
if any items have not been correctly credited.

Designed, produced and printed for Alpha,
an imprint of
SCRIPTURE PRESS FOUNDATION (UK) LTD
Raans Road, Amersham-on-the-Hill, Bucks HP6 6JQ by
Nuprint Ltd, Station Road, Harpenden, Herts AL5 4SE

CONTENTS

Illustrations

INTRODUCTION

The origins and destiny of life are topical subjects. Readers will be surprised at how much science and the Bible reveal about these.

There is much scientific background in the Bible which can only be accounted for if the author of the Bible is the Creator of the universe. In speaking of science, I mean that science which has general concensus of agreement arising out of empirical investigation, not changing theories.

Science now uses popular terms. In answer to the question 'How did we get here?' Oparin (a dedicated Marxist) replied that the first ingredients for life arose out of 'soupy seas' existing in the primeval earth. Dr L. Croft (lecturer in biological science) calls it the 'great soup myth'. The Soviet Union sold that idea to universities around the world by financing science books, so that 'Oparin succeeded in converting most of western society to his belief'. Scientists now believe that the early seas were not soupy.

The origins of life go further back than that. Out in space NASA's space probe found the first ripples of gravity and 'lumps in the primeval soup'. A scientist explained 'that's when the early universe gave a hiccup and we've just heard the echo.' It shows that all things were leading up to man, others have said, to give an earth small enough for his gravity strength, but stars large enough to make his heavier atoms.

Concerning man's origins, popular terms are again

used. The skeleton in Africa suggested as man's origins is not given the long Latin name, but called 'Lucy'.

Cosmic dust was baked in the high pressure cookers of the large hot stars, and scientists now say that man was made of the same dust as the earth.

Does that echo a verse in the Bible, 'God made man of the dust of the earth'?

Tablets, mounds and pottery dug up from older civilisations confirm that all the Biblical dates and history in the Bible are both factual and true.

Above all, the Bible contains God's prophecies of creation through to our future history. God tells the prophets before each stage, all that is to happen, all that will happen and why. In this way God proves that He is unfolding a remarkable plan for the future happiness of the world and for you. This plan could have unfolded without suffering if mankind had not rebelled against God. But know, even by suffering, especially that of Jesus Christ, those purposes will be fulfilled.

How this book can help you

Dr Victor Pearce presents to you this abridged version from three books, *Evidence from Science* (Vol. 1), from *Archaeology* (Vol. 2), and from *Bible Prophecy* (Vol. 3). Many have been denied this knowledge or had it twisted, so please pass it on. Satisfy their heart cry and that of the Lord who expressed his grief over false shepherds who neither care for the sheep nor subtle Satanic deceptions which lead many astray.

What this book can do for you

You will learn that the Bible bears the genetic fingerprints of the Creator. You see that when the Bible dates for sacred history are followed, it harmonises beautifully with the thousands of tablets throughout the Middle East and testifies to the accuracy of Bible history. You will also see how a class of so-called scholars are unwilling to accept this evidence, but cling to their subjective theories formed before archaeology revealed the facts.

Finally, you will see how prophecy makes the Bible relevant today, especially the remarkable fulfilment in contemporary events. It thrills the believer and startles the uninterested into concern. It is the effective answer to Christ's claims because God prepared the prophets for them down the centuries before he came.

The facts which are brought before you in this book, can help to give you a firm, factual faith to face life and the confidence to convince others.

In the Bible you have the most remarkable book in the world, looked at from any angle. It is indeed the double-edged 'sword of the Spirit'. Enjoy reading *Weighing the Evidence*.

1 Science and Truth

The most effective way for you to give evidence to a doubter is to use what science already accepts in the order of creation. Then reveal to him that this correlates with Genesis 1. How did it then get into the Bible in a non-scientific age unless God revealed it?

I quote scientists to show how that new facts are bringing leading scientists back to accept the Creator, and that science shows that mankind was the object of His creation. Scientists call this the 'Anthropic Principle'.

Many doubters have been surprised when I have shown them the British Museum book. *The Succession of Life through Geological Time*, by Oakley and Muir-Wood. I have put the chapter and verses of Genesis down the margin of this science book. The reader can see that the order of events was the same. Green vegetation to supply oxygen, life in the waters, land animals and finally mankind.

Dr Rendle Short made this comment in his book, *Modern Discovery and the Bible:*

> These considerations bring to light a perfectly amazing accordance between the Creation narrative and the discoveries of modern science. When we remember the wild guesses as to the ultimate nature and origin of the earth that were current amongst other ancient people, the accuracy of Genesis stands out in solitary grandeur. Geology is a young science; the classification of strata is not much older than a hundred years; we may be sure the

author of the Creation narrative derived none of his information from fossil hunting. Neither guesswork nor intuition taught the writer to arrange events in the correct order. This narrative bears the marks of a divine inspiration.

CORRELATION OF SCIENCE AND SCRIPTURE

(By giving the order of events, we do not necessarily substantiate the timescale sometimes suggested.)

Science	**Genesis** Chapter 1
Before the days of Creation	
The universe begins with the explosion of the primeval atom	'In the beginning God created the heavens and the earth' v. 1
'Streams of light quanta from...the Big Bang' (Gamov)	'Let there be light' v. 3
Our galaxy begins to rotate	
Pre-Cambrian Eras	
Earth swaddled in thick steamy bands	1st Day begins in darkness v. 5
Condensation into oceans and clouds	2nd Day 'Let an expanse separate the waters from the waters' v. 6
Early Pre-Cambrian Schists with rocks oxidised by chloroplasts and blue-green algae	3rd Day land emerges v. 9 'Let the earth bring forth green' (*deshe*) v. 11
Dense vapours clear to reveal sun, moon and stars	4th Day 'Let there be lights in the sky' v. 14 'God had already made the sun, moon and stars' v. 16
Post-Cambrian Eras	
Marine fossils swarm the strata	5th Day 'Let the waters bring forth swarms of life' v. 20
Insects and angio-sperms	'Winged creatures' v. 20b
Amphibians and Reptiles	'Great sea monsters' v. 21
New Life Eras	
Land animals Age of mammals	6th Day 'Let the earth bring forth living creatures'
Man	6th Day, latter part, 'Let us make man'

2 | Life

The DNA Genetic Life Code

When you have shown an enquirer that the order of events in creation is similar to that which science has discovered, you can then reveal the origin of that order. Genesis says that it was the result of God's spoken word.

Each time God spoke, a new order of life came into being. The DNA genetic code now reveals that all life forms are a result of a code of instructions.

The Cell

So let us look at the cell. I will make it simple because, even if you can master one or two parts of the points, you will give them powerful evidence for creation, because evidence from the cell is very convincing. On the following pages you will see I have outlined (in a diagram and a summary) seven big problems about the cell which modern knowledge presents to one who does not believe in the Creator.

Even if you only master the first two points, they can floor an unbeliever unless they just will not face up to the facts. So don't think you have to digest all eight points at once.

The enzyme which copied the Messenger RNA is created by that copy. It would not exist to copy unless there was an original Creator.

All the editor and sub-editor enzymes exist as a result

of the editing. They would not be there to edit unless there was an original Creator.

The two hundred specialist workers are all made by the machinery they feed. To try and account for their existence, Dr F. Crick asks for frozen miracles.

Then there is the mystery of the translator. Surely the one who knew the translation to put into the code-breaker, must be the same one who composed the DNA code, the Book of Man.

GOD'S AMAZING WORD-PROCESSOR

1. Bible says God created by words.

DNA code demonstrates this, in Genesis 1, God speaks eight times (Ps 33:6,9; Ps,139:16; Heb. 1:3; Col. 1:15–17; Jn. 1:1–3; Rev. 22:13). Each time God spoke, a new order resulted. All life consists of cells which are operated by the DNA code.

2. DNA instructions to man.

What Psalm 139:16 calls God's book, is now called 'Book of Man' (Human Genome). Chromosomes = volumes; Gene clusters = chapters; Genes = sentences. Cystic fibrosis is copy error in book seven, chapter five, paragraph three, sentence nine. Over a million pages needed for all human instructions.

3. In all cells of living creatures.

The cell is a computerised factory. A 'fax copier' taking instructions from the master hard copy. This (M.RNA) is sub-edited by eight sub-editors. They use God's genetic engineering enzymes, for tracing, cutting, rejoining and glueing.

Edited copies (Transfer RNA) are used by workers (200 types) to feed into 20,000 translating machines (ribosomes). Only God could have known translation.

Ribosomes obey instructions and produce protein chains. These make body organs and tissues.

Code changed to alphabet of 64 'letters'.

4. Mitochondrion fuel producer.

To work cell's machinery.

Has female copyright and monopoly DNA.

Therefore scientists know that everybody is descended from one mother (Gen. 3:20). 'Eve mother of all living'.

5. Seven problems face the atheist.

The Code's origin, code breaker, fax copier, enzyme sub-editors, machine operators, the fuel factory, and meiosis cell division. Each of these are interdependent upon the other. The factory has to be complete to work.

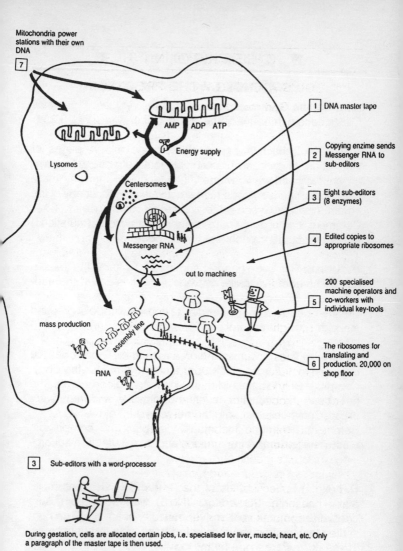

During gestation, cells are allocated certain jobs, i.e. specialised for liver, muscle, heart, etc. Only a paragraph of the master tape is then used.

Fig 1 Cell's Automated Factory

EVIDENCE OF THE CREATOR

Here are the *eight big problems for the agnostic or atheist.*
Check each number with that on the cell drawing, Fig. 3.2.

A. (No.1) The DNA code requires one million pages of
instruction, gives complicated technical instructions to make
an animal or man. They are more technical that any man-
made computerised code to make an airliner etc. or any of the
computers of the world—the brain is as complicated.
Comment: could a series of faults in instructions (mutations)
make, by accident, such a technical code?

B. (No.6) This code needed someone who knew the translation and made a machine to translate it. It is called the ribosome.
Comment: someone was needed to know the code secret and
make the code breaker.

C. (No.6) The ribosomes are on an assembly line to obey the
decoded instructions and to produce the parts for the body.
Complicated machines like the non-stop blood-pump (the
heart) and the circulatory system of pipes to and from every
organ. Some cells become the nerve system of the brain.
Comment: it needed technically complex and compatable
machinery to read off instructions and to manufacture accord-
ingly.

D. (No.4) Edited copies of the instructions are sent out to
every ribosome. Sub-editors (No.3) with word-processors
specialised to make either liver, muscle, heart, etc. The right
sentence of instruction is selected to send to the ribosomes.
These editors are made by the cell factory.
Comment: they are made by the cell, but the cell cannot
make them until they are made, because they are part of its
machinery.

E. (No.5) Two hundred different specialised workers, or enzymes attend the production machines (ribosomes). These are all made by the cell factory.

Comment: Dr Francis Crick said that these were '200 frozen miracles'. The cell cannot make them unless they already exist to make them.

F. (No.7) The Fuel and Power department, or Mitochondria supplies fuel for every working machine (organelle) in the cell. It supplies fuel in three grades—one star, two star and three star. This power station is as complicated as any made by man.

Comment: it needs the fuel it produces to start its own fuel producing machinery to make fuel. Who produced the first fuel?

G. When a cell itself has become specialised during gestation it becomes part of the brain, heart, or blood cell, etc. the centresomes (No.8) multiply it into those cells and it is directed to become part of that organ in the right part of the body.

Comment: who provided the three-dimensional blueprint for correct positioning?

---

3 | Lumps in the Primeval Soup

There was great excitement among the scientists when the NASA space probe sent back pictures of the first ripples in the universe. 'Wow! What an exciting discovery,' said one scientist from Durham. What caused those ripples? It was the force of gravity. Scientists use funny language today. They said, 'There were lumps in the primeval soup!' Yes, that is how they put it—'lumps in the primeval soup!' And do you know what some of those scientists said?

> The strength of gravity shows that it was intended to lead up to man. Man was in mind. Why? Because 'the strength of gravity was just the right strength for the size of the earth to support man.' Dr Nigel Calder said, 'For man to walk on this planet with 12,000 kilometres of the earth beneath his feet, man had to have the two gravity balances in his head rightly tuned.'

Many scientists call this 'The Anthropic Principle'. Isaiah 45:12 puts this principle in a nutshell. I quote, 'God said, I made the earth and created man upon it.' Those first ripples had man in mind. It was written into the space-time plan!

Leading Scientists confirm the Bible

Is this the Word that God spoke when he said, 'Let there be light'? Two leading world scientists say it is. Le Maître the mathematician who first worked it all out, said this: 'Let there be light? correctly described the origin of the universe'. That other leading physicist, Professor Geoge Gamov, said that the Divine command, 'Let there be light!' was completely scientific. Here are his words: 'All the chemical elements which we deal with today must have been formed within the first 30 minutes of the life of this universe, and it accords with the Divine command, "Let there be light". There certainly was light through this intense radiation.'

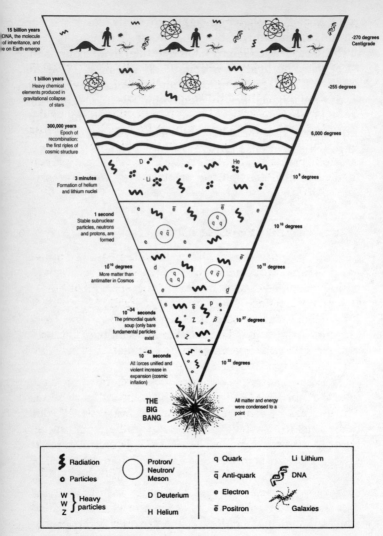

Fig 2 The Big Bang Theory

LUMPS IN THE PRIMEVAL SOUP ◀

NASA Spacecraft Discovery

I stated before that many secular scientists are now admitting that the way matter and gravity was formed in the early universe indicates that it had man in mind. This is, of course, what the Bible says as well.

Since the discovery of the ripples in outer space by the NASA probe, people are asking, 'Why are the scientists so excited about this discovery in the universe?'

Well, it was to the American Physical Society meeting, early in 1992, that the satellite discovery was presented.

Quark Soups in Six Flavours

I like the popular cookery terms the scientists used about the thin gruel at the beginning of creation coalescing into a lumpy soup soon after creation. This space probe gave the first evidence that it had actually happened. Dr Michael Turner said the discovery was, 'The Holy Grail of Cosmology'. The satellite had sent back pictures of the ripples which were forming into matter. The Bible adds that it was God who was doing it.

Another scientist asks, 'But how did the lumps get into the porridge?'—to use a different culinary term. The matter of which the earth is made and of which your body is made, was formed by gravity pulling together all kinds of primary particles. Science has been finding that matter is more complex than anyone thought. At one time, matter was thought to consist only of protons, electrons and neutrons, but this soup, as the analogist has called it, consists of lots of simpler elements called quarks. What that satellite has discovered is the formation of quark soup to make up the material needed for galaxies and planets of life.

There are different kinds of quarks with interacting

forces to hold things together. There are 36 different kinds of quarks in the universe's quark soup.

There are up quarks, down quarks, charmed quarks, strange quarks, top quarks and bottom quarks. All these in turn have anti-quarks, anti-ups, downs, tops and bottoms and so on. This is all to keep matter from falling apart. Do you remember what Colossians 1:17 says, that 'God created all things by Jesus by whom all things hold together'.

▼ CHECKPOINTS ▼

NASA SPACE PROBE

1. **NASA Feedback** was like a video run backwards catching up with the beginning of the universe. Revelation 20:11 describes a 'Big Bang', but God causes it. Gamov and Le Maitre who worked it out, quoted Genesis 1:3 'Let there be light'.

   Scientists use culinery terms:
   - First elementary particles were like 'thin gruel'.
   - 'Ripples' proved gravity operating (lumps in the quark soup).
   - 'Universe hiccuped and NASA heard the echo'.

2. **Man centred: strength of gravity proved man was in mind**
   - Anthropic principle—required small earth but big stars. Why? Any planet bigger than earth would crush man. Yet huge stars needed to fuse the quarks into atoms, required for man's body. These novae stars then exploded the dust into space for man's body (and planets).
   - Professor Calder (BBC science broadcaster) says, 'Gravity detectors in man's head'...are rightly adjusted for earth's mass. Anthropic principle supported by lead-

ing scientists. Isaiah 45:12, 'I made the earth and created man upon it.'

- DNA acids for man created in the hot interiors of explod-
ing stars. St John was overawed that he had touched the
'Word of Life' (1 Jn. 1:1).

3. Reality is invisible Scientists find that what is detectable
in whole universe is only 1%. The other 99% is invisible.
'The worlds were framed by the activating word (hreemati)
of God, so that the things which are seen were not made by
the visible.' (Heb. 11:3).

Stephen Hawking of Cambridge is attempting to combine
Quantam Physics with Relativity to give a Theory of Everything. He wonders whether we shall know everything without the mind of God. Solution: the mind of God is given in
his Word (Heb. 1:1).

Note: Quantam Physics
Primary elements are 36 quarks in 6 flavours and 3 colours.
Relativity is $E = mc^2$

4 | Fossils

Imaginary Stooping Apemen

What picture does the discovery of more fossils give in regard to so-called apemen? The trend in man-like skeletons is to show that there were no apemen links between true man and the ape. This may surprise you because of all the propaganda which you get. For example, in Amsterdam, I saw posters showing apemen gradually walking more and more upright. In actual fact, no such skeletons have been found.

Fig 3 Row of Stooping Apes

An article written in the *New Scientist* actually laments this fact. It is written by Dr M. Pickford of Oxford. He takes evolution for granted, only lamenting that, as regards to man, there is no evidence to support it. Here is what he says: 'The fossil void is particularly frustrating because it was during this time that the earliest human ancestor embarked on a vital stage in its journey towards humanity.' The fossil void he speaks of is the absence of apemen. But that is what begs the whole question.

Powerful Fossil Evidence

Some have asserted that the succession of fossils in the rocks has been falsely concocted on an evolutionary assumption. This is not correct. The fossil record was discovered by geologists a long time before Darwin launched his theory.

Indeed, the fossil record was evidence against evolution. Even Darwin acknowledged this!

For Christians, untrained in geology, to attack the fossil record is like shooting themselves in the foot and making themselves ineffective for battle.

▼ CHECKPOINTS ▼

MISSING MISSING LINKS

Science supports Genesis' order of life's appearance:

1. But each order appears suddenly. Are there any links? Darwin admitted that unless links were found, the fossils supported a series of special creations.

   Those links have not been found. Fossil scientists, Coffin and Anderson, say, '...even more like creative acts than in Darwin's day. Not gaps in fossil records found, only absence of link fossils.'

2. Six new theories have been presented by scientists: explosive evolution; saltation leaps; reptile lays bird's egg; hopeful monster theory; neo-Darwinism by mutations; punctuated equilibria.

3. Mendel's genetics also brought in a new problem for

Darwinism. Darwin thought trait attained in life could be passed to offspring. But genetics showed that only characteristics in the genes were inherited.

4. Imaginary Apemen.
Fictional drawings abound. All quadrapedals or upright-walking.
Meet Lucy 'Beginning of humankind'.
Fossil void between ape and man lamented by Johanson and Edey who found 'Lucy', and Dr M. Pickford.

5. Don't shoot your foot. Make fossils your friend. Some Christians dump good evidence. Geological succession discovered 50 years before Darwin. Overlaps reverse some fossils.

The Absence of Link Fossils

Today, many scientists are having a re-think, and in any case the old Darwinian model has been greatly modified by two factors. Firstly, our knowledge of Mendel's genetics and Crick's DNA demonstrates that nothing can happen in a species which does not happen in its DNA genes. Secondly, it has become plain that new and higher orders appear in groups comparatively suddenly. Consequently, some have called it 'explosive evolution', a seeming contradiction in terms.

It would be better to associate these appearances with each of the times that God spoke the creative words. In other words such complicated creatures were the result of re-coding of DNA, the language of life, when the dramatically advanced orders appear, such as vertebrates, amphibians, reptiles, birds, mammals and man.

Life Appears Suddenly

The overall picture is that of a series of jumps to major new types of animals. It is not now sufficient to excuse ourselves by saying that we merely need to look for more fossils. That has been done, yet the picture is the same.

This is really a death blow to Darwinism, and so evolutionary scientists have come up with a succession of alternatives. There have been five new theories all succeeding each other, because none of them is satisfactory even to evolutionists.

Professor Sir Fred Hoyle and Professor C. Wickramasinghe, eminent Cambridge scientists, reflect the change: 'Contrary to Darwin's theory...evolution on earth was a series of leaps.' The fossil picture gives a pattern of the major groups of new advanced animals appearing together. Between them and their assumed ancestors, there is a lack of linking fossils to show evolutionary progress. This is a consistent story throughout the fossil record.

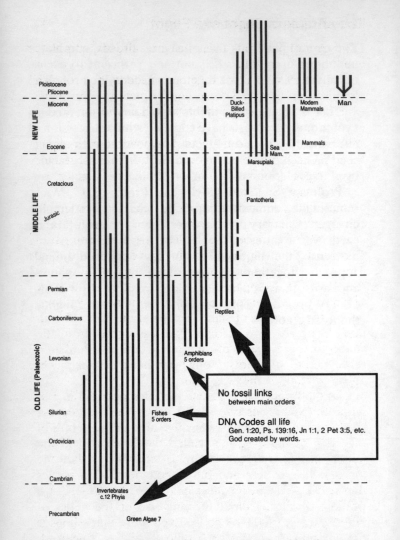

Fig 4 Fossil record life, showing the sequence in which the seven main orders of life appear

The following labels appear within the figure:

NEW LIFE

MIDDLE LIFE

OLD LIFE (Palaeozoic)

Ploistocene
Pliocene
Miocene
Eocene
Cretacious
Jurasic
Permian
Carboniferous
Levonian
Silurian
Ordovician
Cambrian
Precambrian

Duck-Billed Platipus
Modern Mammals
Man
Sea Mam.
Mammals
Marsupials
Pantotheria
Reptiles
Amphibians 5 orders
Fishes 5 orders
Invertebrates c.12 Phyia
Green Algae 7

No fossil links
between main orders

DNA Codes all life
Gen. 1:20, Ps. 139:16, Jn 1:1, 2 Pet 3:5, etc.
God created by words.

36 FOSSILS ◄

The Miracle of Sight and Flight

Did your camera fall from heaven, already complete with batteries and film?

Did your TV set come together accidentally through a storm sweeping into your house or was it a hurricane which blew all the components together with the screws in place?

A man on TV said that this was possible concerning the eye, the human eye. It could all have come together. How? By a series of a million accidents selected by environment.

Actually, your camera and TV set are very simple compared with the complexity of the human eye. The automatic focusing of the camera is simple compared with the very much finer focusing of your iris and lens. The little colour spots on your TV screen only number a few thousand. Compare that with the retina at the back of your eye. Your eye has 20 million nerve endings taking the message of sight to your brain. Yes, 20 million. Your TV set can only read the signals from the studio by a rapid shut off and on system to stimulate a succession of still shots. Your brain has a similar mechanism to read the moving picture.

Did God intend man to use the telescope and microscope to explore his universe? I believe he did because the human eye has a very sensitive area in the centre of the back of the eye. It is called the fovea and in the middle of that is an even more sensitive area called the macula. It is so fine and full of communication nerves that it can read the smallest image. Without these, we would know little about the universe or the genes of inheritance in the DNA code. Even more marvellous is the creation of all this each time a child is conceived, because the instructions for it are contained in the cell's genetic code.

▼ CHECKPOINTS ▼

THE GREAT TV COVER-UP

TV propaganda for evolution hides present scientists' doubts.

Barren rocks before *sudden creation* of twelve phyla of marine life.

As Genesis 1:20 says, 'God said, let waters swarm with moving creatures'. The Cambrian strata has swarms of fossils—suddenly. David Attenborough on TV said there must have been soft-bodied creatures earlier which left no fossils. But soft bodies *do* leave fossils. Sea urchins of the Cambrian period are still similar today.

Flying aeronautical marvels of four different kingdoms of animals.

All contrary to survival of fittest theory:
1. Insects (preceded by metamorphosis in cocoon) [Amber evidence].
2. Reptiles 'practised swift runs and leaps for thousands of years until they could fly' (*Encyclopaedia Britannica*)!
3. Birds: mechanism of interlocking feathers quite different from scales.
4. Mammals like bats—no fossils of mice changing into bats.

No evolutionary record of any of these. Professor Fred Hoyle found Archaeopterix to be a fraud.

Genesis 1:21 God created every winged creature.
Job 39:13 God created the peacock's wings.
Job 38:26 Migration of birds by God's wisdom.

Sight: from first fossils, all have eyes, even worms:
      sonic sight for bats (dark caves).
      telescopic sight for eagles.
      trilobites had complex eye for opaque deep water.
      Octopus eyes like human's (yet entirely different kingdom).
      "He who made the eye, shall he not see?" (Ps. 94:9)
      human eye: 20 million nerves from retina to brain.
      automatic focusing and light metre of iris and lens.

Twenty-two British Museum biologists said in 1981 'Evolution is not a fact'.

5 | Darwin's Second Thoughts

Fig 5 Cartoon of Charles Darwin

The other objection we must deal with is that Darwin 'never recanted any of his scientific views'. However, the following report was published in the *Bromley and Kentish Times* with the recollections of a Mr A.H. Nicholls who was closely acquainted with the servants of Darwin's household who had nursed him through his final illness:

... this lady who had been in attendance on Darwin prior to his death had informed him that he requested her to read the New Testament to him and asked her to arrange for the Sunday School children to sing, 'There is a green hill far away'. This was done and Darwin, who was greatly moved, said, 'How I wish I had not expressed my theory of evolution as I have done.'

It is probable that the 'lady who nursed Darwin', was Mrs Evans. She had been with the Darwin household as a nurse for many years and as she was a member of the Gospel Hall congregation, she could have easily arranged for the Sunday School to sing an Easter hymn for Darwin.

DARWIN'S CONVERSION

1. **Darwin's conversion reported by Lady Hope. Who was she?**
   - (a) Daughter of General Sir Arthur Cotton
   - (b) Wife of Admiral Sir James Hope
   - (c) Author of 37 books (British Library)
   - (d) Temperance worker

2. **Also reported by:**
   - (a) James Fegan, evangelist, temperance advocate
   - (b) Ishmael Jones in *Christian Herald* periodical
   - (c) Booth Tucker of Salvation Army
   - (d) A N Nichols who also heard Darwin's regrets about evolution.

3. **Mission conversions on Darwin's lawn reported by:**
   - (a) Darwin's wife Emma
   - (b) Darwin's butler
   - (c) *Bromley and Kentish Times*

4. **Accuracy confirmed by:**
   - (a) Sir H. Atkins, President of Royal College of Surgeons
   - (b) Darwin's reference to harmonium and summer-house meetings
   - (c) Darwin's letter to evangelist Mr J. Fegan
   - (d) Dr L. R. Croft of Salford University

5. **Darwin:**
   - (a) Regretted the results of his theory
   - (b) Regretted use made by Karl Marx, etc.
   - (c) Regretted use made by Haeckel
   - (d) Admitted that fossil record looked like special creation
   - (e) Made regular donations to South American Missionary Society

God's Timing of Creation Events

An Assessment of Prevailing Views

It is helpful to realise that there have been fashions of interpretation among Bible-believing scientists when it comes to relating Genesis and science. By Bible-believing scientists, I mean scientists who believe that the Bible is fully inspired by the Holy Spirit and therefore is true and accurate in all that it says. The term I shall use for such a person is 'Biblical scientist'.

Earth Days or Galaxy Days?

'And there was evening and there was morning—the first day.' 'And there was evening and there was morning—the second day' (Gen. 1:5,8 NIV).

It is important to understand that the correlation between the creation story and science is not dependent upon whether we regard these days as earth days of 24 hours or cosmic days of geological ages. The fact that the succession of events both physical and biological is similar, stands indisputable. The timing factor is a separate issue.

First we note that the days of creation do not commence until after the initial cosmic events, 'in the beginning'.

> All the heavens, ie. the universe in its earlier stages, were created before the days began to be recorded so that no time scale can be assessed from the Genesis

account, except that it was from the beginning onwards. This is followed by void and darkness of verse 2, into which many primeval processes can be fitted. The days following are then measured by the end of one day the beginning of the next. It is the end which marks the first day—a significance you should note.

Concerning the time factor, I now give a summary of attempts to correlate the days of creation with the findings of science.

▼ CHECKPOINTS ▼

GOD'S TIMING AND HUMAN ASSUMPTIONS

Order of creation is more important than the length of time. Don't insist on voicing your pet time schedule!

Five Fashions of Biblical Scientists

1. Age-Day theory for creation days
In the 19th century most Biblical scientists accepted age-days. Founders of Creation Science Movement accepted this theory, as Dr David Rosevear said. Many in it now press for 24-hour days of creation. Founders and supporters of the Age-Day theory were Dr M. Davies, D. Dewar, Professor Ambrose Fleming, Professor F.A. Filby, Dr R.E.D. Clark, W. Beasley, Professor Rendle-Short.

2. 1000-year days then became popular
Adam lived nearly a thousand-year day. Cf. Genesis 2:17 (RSV).
According to Usshur, six millenial days have passed.
Seventh millenial day of rest and Christ's reign is near, 2 Peter 3:8.

3. Revelation to Moses took six days
Advocated by Professor D. Wiseman, Assyriologist (London University)

Accords with ancient Middle East methods
Professor Van der Spuy similar 'six-day blueprint of billion-year programme'.

4. Galaxy Days 360 million years long
Galaxy takes 360 million years to revolve. Dust across axis makes it go dark every revolution. Genesis 'It was dark. It was light, the second day' (light before the sun).

5. 24-hour Days based on Exodus 20:11
Professor Enoch says sun created *after* the earth. This misinterprets Hebrew historic tense on fourth day. 'God had made sun'. Difficult sixth day afternoon, when ten major events took place. Note that seventh day did not end (Gen. 2:1-3). Hebrews 4 says God still rests.

Essentials: believe God's Words to be true, but don't cause divisions over creation timing (1 Cor. 13:2).

---

7 | The Garden of Eden Discovered

Where did farming begin? Archaeology has traced the geographical centre right back to where the Bible says. At first they looked at other places thinking that farming started there—Europe, then Egypt, then Palestine, then the fertile crescent of the Middle East. If they had looked at where the Bible said it started, they would have saved a lot of wasted time.

In Genesis 2, the exact location and topography of the Garden of Eden are described. You will find them in Genesis 2:10–14. It was in the headwaters of the four rivers, Pison, Gihon, Tigris and Euphrates. These rivers rise on the plateau heights of Eastern Turkey.

Some have different ideas about where the Garden of Eden was. Some have said it was in Mesopotamia, or even in the delta of the Persian Gulf at the mouths of the Tigris and Euphrates rivers.

Don't be deceived by 'Tourist Ideas', or comments by amateurs who have done no empirical research. There is a clear geographical location given in Genesis 2:10–14.

Flannery, in a symposium of world prehistoric archaeologists, draws attention to dry farming by the early farmers. At Ali Kosh 9,500 years ago, cereals were planted in swamp conditions. The small early dry farming village on the Kozistan steppe of south-west Iran, also produced 10,000 identifiable bones from 35 species of domesticated animals. A typical dry farming garden is shown in Fig. 7.

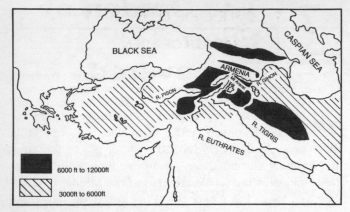

Fig 6 The headwaters of four rivers rising in the Ararat and Armenian mountain ranges

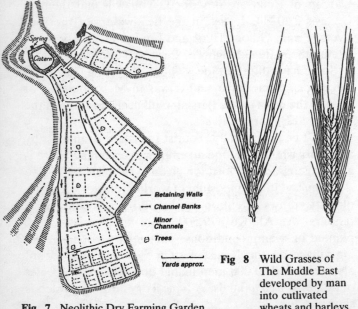

— Retaining Walls
— Channel Banks
--- Minor Channels
⌷ Trees

Yards approx.

Fig 7 Neolithic Dry Farming Garden

Fig 8 Wild Grasses of The Middle East developed by man into cutlivated wheats and barleys

▼ CHECKPOINTS ▼

GARDEN OF EDEN

1. Where?
Source of four rivers, therefore highlands of Western Turkey, not Mesopotamian valley. 'Eden' means plateau.

Lake Van: source of rivers Pison into Black Sea, Gihon into Caspian, Tigris and Euphrates into Persian Gulf.

Evidence: pollen core samples
Archaeological succession (pottery, etc.)
World Conference of Archaeologists.

2. Origin of farming
Where Bible says Adam started. Genesis 2:8,15

- Dry farming techniques—no rain. Genesis 2:6. 'ed' = water not mist. cf Pueblo-style dry farming or 'flood water farming'.
- Flint tools before metals of Genesis 4:22. Adam's tool kit.
- First domestication. God brought animals to Adam. Thirty-five species at Ali-Kosh.
- Cereals native to that area. Wheat, Barley, Legumes.

3. Migration to World. (Evidence: stone axes, digging sticks)
Europe: along Danube, and Mediterranean shores.

East: India, China Yellow River (reaping knives) to America (Bering Straits).

South: Sahara desert lush vegetation (before Flood), Africa.

4. Tablets Genesis 2:4 onwards is *not* a second creation account.
Toledot tablet method v. 4 sums up before sequel is added.

Higher critics did not know this, and still ignore archaeological evidence.

Two names for God on one tablet source was common usage 2,500BC (Ebla tablets use Lord and God together, ie. Yah and El).

8 | Anthropology Supports the Bible

T he theories of anthropology have also been re-
versed, largely through Professor Evans-Pritchard's
insistence on fieldwork.

> Whereas before the 1930s, an evolutionary concept of
> religion was that it developed from animism and magic to
> polytheism and then finally to monotheism, fieldwork
> reversed this and anthropologists now realise that belief
> in one Creator God preceded all other religious con-
> cepts. This gradually corrupted to polytheism, and finally
> to the placating of an extensive array of nature spirits.
> Some popular lecturers in theology seem unaware of this
> change and continue to reshuffle the Old Testament
> documentary-wise, changing its story of one God reveal-
> ing himself into an evolutionary process of man's groping
> from animism to monotheism. In this way many ordi-
> nands and clergy are being persuaded to forsake the
> claims of scripture that God has uniquely revealed him-
> self through the Torah and the prophets and finally
> through the Christ.

Fieldwork Evidence for Primitive Belief in One God

These people believed in a High God Creator. These
'World Views', as anthropologists call them, are quite
abstract in their concepts. Dr Pospisil, living among the
Kapauki in 1954 reported, 'This stone age tribe was not
without its abstract philosophy. God is omniscient, omni-

potent, and omnipresent, credited with the creation of all things and with having determined all events.'

▼ CHECKPOINTS ▼

EVIDENCE FOR FALL

1. Wickedness gradually increases:
First pioneers along Danube needed no fortifications.
Second Danubians fortified. Earth gods, suggestive figurines.
First stone-age city had no such figurines (Gen. 6:4) and no warfare.
Oral tradition from primitives of age of innocence, eg. China Miao, Andamanese, New Guinea Kanpauki, Australian Aboriginal folklore, First American Indians. Universal original belief in Creator, 'Sky God', before polytheism and animism.

2. Sin-offerings commence.
Abel's sacrifice. Genesis 4:2-5.
- Increase in lamb bones in Shanidar-Zarzi complex, Karim Shahir, Bolt Cave, Jarmo, Ali Kosh.
- Worldwide primitive custom of propitiation.
Professor Zwemer: eg. Eskimos, Pygmies, Algonguins Bushmen, and Veddas.
Professor Evans-Pritchard: Nuer tribe, Upper Nile, confession over ox.
- Bible evidence. Tribes always degenerated from original revelation eg.,
Cains descendants. Tower of Babel.
Abraham's relatives. (Lot and Ammonites, Moabites)
Jacob's descendants: Esau and Edomites, then Israel and Judah sacrificed children to demon gods.
Then idolatry into the medieval church as prophesied.

Romans 1:28. 'Did not retain God in their knowledge and degenerated into immorality, wickedness, greed, murder, hatred of God.' Translated from the Greek text.

Learn Romans 3:23; 5:12 and 5:8.

---

9 The Five Books of Moses

The first section of scripture is the Pentateuch or the five books of Moses: Genesis, Exodus, Leviticus, Numbers and Deuteronomy. It tells us of Creation, man's rebellion against God, the Flood, God's choice of a nation through which the Saviour of mankind would come, the deliverance of that nation from slavery, the giving of God's Laws and the way of atonement. The whole section was and still is called the Torah or Law; in fact that is scripture's name for it. From the first synagogues even unto today, the Torah is kept in scroll form in a beautifully made cabinet in the holiest place of the synagogue which is called the Ark.

We must remember that Moses lived in the greatest period of Israelite history. He it was who led Israel out of the slavery of Egypt. It would have been strange if he had made no record of such events, especially as every monument of Egypt in his time depicted scribes recording every event, even routine daily agricultural processes. That Moses also had the habit of recording current history is seen in Deuteronomy 31:22, 'Moses wrote this song the same day'. Other references to Moses' writing is in Exodus 17:8–14; 24:4,7; 34:4; Numbers 33:2; Deuteronomy 31:9–12, 24–26. Moreover, Numbers 33:2 tells us that Moses methodically recorded all the travels of his 40 years' leadership.

That a regular account was kept seems to be the point of the remark in Exodus 17:14, 'Write this for a memorial in The Book', (translated from Hebrew) as though there was a regular account kept in a well-known book.

Further evidence for Moses
There is now strong evidence that Moses did write the first five books of the Bible as was originally believed. These books are called the Pentateuch or Torah.

Course Material in Error

Experts have since found that the literary methods evident in the Pentateuch are those of the time of Moses and not of a later date when methods changed. Experts in this practical field are Professor Kenneth Kitchen, Professor of Archaeology and Oriental Studies; Dr D. Wiseman, Professor of Assyriology and a Semitist; and Professor Alan Millard. All have recognised international standing.

Professor Kitchen himself has translated tablets and scripts from treaties in Hittite, Elamite, Sumerian, Aramaic languages as well as Egyptian, Ugaritic, Akkadian, etc.

In a typical Course for Lay Readers in one diocese there was no mention of their scholarly, factual findings, and so I have been asked to supply this lack. Neither was any mention made of up-to-date scholars who have taught in theological colleges such as J.A. Motyer; Dr John Wenham; Dr W.J. Martin; Donald Robinson; Professor F.F. Bruce; A. Gibson; Bishop John Robinson; R.T. France and others.

These experts found that ancient tablets and scripts used both divine names in their accounts, sometimes together and sometimes singly according to the subject material. They did not indicate different authorship or sources.

The old-fashioned Higher Critics did not know this, so they divided up the Bible stories according to the name used for God. By doing this, they made the one version into two or three versions, and by doing so they artificially created contradictory versions.

▼ CHECKPOINTS ▼

UNDERSTANDING THE STYLE

Professor Kitchen of Liverpool University, School of Archaeology and Oriental Studies, gives some examples showing that the Covenant in Exodus to Deuteronomy is set out on the same principles of the Hittite covenant: 'Much information on covenants and treaties in the Near East has come to light. From no less than 25 treaties from the archives of the Hittites, Ugarit, etc., it has been possible to establish the clear pattern'. This is:

1. The author of the Covenant (Jehovah)
2. Reference to earlier relations (Patriarchs)
3. Basic stipulations (Ten Commandments) followed by more details (Ex. 21 to Num. 10)
4. Arrangement for deposit of the Covenant in the vassal's sanctuary (recorded only in Deut. 31:24–25)
5. Periodic reading of the Covenant terms to the people (recorded only in Deut.)
6. Witnesses (Ex. 24) sealed by sprinkling the blood of the Covenant
7. Curses for disobedience to the Covenant and blessing for keeping it (Lev. 26 and Deut. 30)
8. Oath of obedience with solemn ceremony

This is also fully documented by V. Korosec of Leipzig and G.E. Mendenhall (Oxford Ashmoleum Museum).

MOSES IN A TIME MACHINE

In an imaginary six day space-time journey, we see how God created the universe and man, male and female. If space and time are relative, it avoids conceptual difficulties; so we speed back with NASA probe to see God actually creating the universe and how it all accords with Genesis and we converse with Moses as he writes it down!

The Sixth Day has the longest programme

In it Moses sets down the blueprint for the following busy schedule:

1. God made the land animals from the ground.
2. God created Adam from the dust and nuclear acids left by supernovae.
3. God planted the garden of Eden and made trees and plants to grow.
4. God placed Adam in the garden to cultivate it.
5. God told Adam not to eat the forbidden fruit.
6. God brought all the animals and birds to Adam to be named.
7. God put Adam into a deep sleep and removed a rib.
8. From a cell in his rib, by genetic engineering, he built the cell into a woman.
9. Introduces Adam to her who exclaims 'At long last one made flesh from my flesh!' (cells from my cells).
10. They were joined as husband and wife and became 'one flesh'.
11. God told Adam and Eve to populate the earth and subdue it.

It is exciting to watch the operations with the knowledge we now have of the seven enzymes for genetic engineering.

Why not send for my audio-cassette from 13, Lismore Road, Eastbourne, England.

Cain's Wife

'Cain lay with his wife and she conceived and bare Enoch' (Gen. 4:17). 'After Seth was born (when Adam was 130 years old), Adam lived 800 years and had other sons and daughters' (Gen. 5:4).

As the reference comes after the statement that Cain had migrated eastwards, some have asked where did Cain find a wife? Cain's wife could have been one of his sisters—for Adam and Eve had daughters as well as sons (Gen. 5:4) one of whom he may have married before he became a fugitive. Cain feared others when he said, 'I shall be a fugitive and wanderer in the earth and whosoever finds me will kill me.' Who would these other men be? By the time Adam and Eve were 130 years old (Gen. 5:3), they would have lived long enough for their children's descendants to have increased to a population as large as 3,000,000 and to have travelled some distance.

We should not suppose that Catal Hüyük is the actual city Cain built for, as we have seen, where Cain fled from his homeland, he is said to have travelled 'eastward from Eden' (Gen. 4:16 RSV) and dwelt in the land of Nod.

But the discovery of Catal Hüyük does give us sound archaeological evidence that the Bible was right and that Cain and his contemporaries were capable of building cities in the New Stone Age.

CAIN'S CITY

1. **New Stone Age City** Genesis 4:17 was before metals in 4:22.
   Catal Hüyük on Turkish Plateau discovered by Professor J.
   Mellaart
   Before this discovery, some thought Bible wrong to speak
   of cities before the Bronze age, because a city needed
   specialised trades to support it, and organisation

2. **Catal Hüyük, 8,000 population** had trades, and market
   gardening outside
   Traded volcanic glass tools for miles around, carpentry
   with flint tools
   Weaving and dye-stamped cloth. Frescoes showed
   women in long dresses, and men in loin-cloth or skirt down
   to knees. Leopard skin caps

3. **Levels three and four** (five generations after Cain)
   Pictures of *pipes and harps* (Gen. 4:17–21)
   Copper-stone Age arrives, but not smelting
   'Tubal-Cain was a *hammerer* of copper and iron' (Gen. 4:22)
   Hebrew means hammerer. Smelting of iron not until 1500BC

4. **Technological background** to Bible 10,000 to 1,500BC is
   remarkable
   New Stone Age, Copper-stone Age, Bronze Age, Iron Age.
   Succession all correct

5. **Population explosion** as in Genesis 6. Other city mounds
   in sight.
   In 130 years (Gen. 5:3) computer estimates population at 3
   million.

6. **Religion Hüyük** was very religious, but astray from truth
   One in three rooms were shrines to mother goddess
   Cain had refused lamb atonement (Gen. 4:5; Heb. 11:4)

10 | Oceans Rush Over Continents

The deep oceans would have rushed over the continents, swept animals into caves and even up mountains to beat their bones into broken bits and pieces.

> This immense volume of water would flood out of its ocean beds like water jerked out of a swirling wash basin. No wonder the tablets found in the Middle East say, 'The Flood came up'—came up from the waters of the deep oceans. No wonder the Bible and the archaelogical tablets say that, as a result, all flesh died.
>
> It was a catastrophe bigger than the world has ever known.

The comparatively new science of Palaeomagnetism shows that the earth has turned on a different pole in earlier times—probably where the magnetic pole is now. The geographic pole is now about 16 degrees away from the magnetic pole.

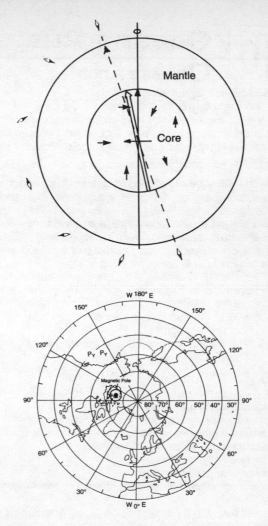

Fig 9 Diagrams to illustrate the effects of the change of the magnetic axis in causing the submersion of certain lands

▼ CHECKPOINTS ▼

NOAH'S FLOOD

1. Flood caused by a Change of Axis
Palaeomagnetism of rocks proves it.
Magnetic poles caused by independent inner core revolution.
Outer crust geographical pole once aligned with the core.
Sudden realignment caused huge surge of seawater sufficient
to cover the land for a time.

2. Effect of Change of Axis would be a worldwide flood
Water stationary on old poles would have to speed up to
300mph.
Oceans at old equator would swirl at an angle to new equator.
Oceans are three times as deep as mountains.
Oceans cover over twice as much of globe as land.
Oceans would swirl out of the deep as in:
Genesis 7:7 'Fountains of the great deep burst out'.
Psalm 104:6–9 'The waters (from the deep) stood above the
mountains...They may not again cover the earth'. (RSV)
Job 38:12–15 Sun rose in new place 'to shake the wicked
out of their new earth'.
2 Peter 3:5,6 Flood from around continents.
Matthew 24:39 'Swept them away'.
God tells Job the earth is like a cylinder seal which turns on a
spindle.

3. Evidence of Axis change
New sea levels throughout the world. Fossil beaches.
Oceans were higher at old equator—centrifugal bulge. Fossil
beach through Andes 12,000 feet high.
Coral beds at an angle.
Mountain ranges at an angle.
Palaeomagnetism indicates big change in 'recent' human his-
tory.
Nations testify to a different pole star, ie. Anaxagorus and St.
Peter (2 Pet. 3:6,7).

The Flood Beyond Doubt

As Andre Parrot, the famous French archaeologist, points out, it is difficult to doubt that such detailed and persistent records have a factual basis. 'There can be no question that the Flood marked a clear break in history,' he writes. 'The memory of it remained vividly in men's minds as well in Mesopotamia as in Palestine.' And again, 'The cataclysm was accompanied by destuction on such a scale, and made such an impression, that it became one of the themes of cuneiform literature.'

Genesis: the Original Version

There is, in all this, little conception of God's grief at the sin of mankind as in Genesis 6:5–14. These are the type of details which would be unpopular and get left out of later secular accounts.

> The Lord saw that the wickedness of man was great in the earth, and that every imagination of the thoughts of his heart was only evil continually. And the Lord was sorry that he had made man on the earth, and it grieved him to his heart. So the Lord said, 'I will blot out man whom I have created from the face of the ground, man and beast and creeping things and birds of the air, for I am sorry that I have made them.' But Noah found favour in the eyes of the Lord. Noah was a righteous man, blameless in his generation; Noah walked with God. And Noah had three sons, Shem, Ham, and Japheth. Now the earth was corrupt in God's sight, and the earth was filled with violence. And God saw the earth, and behold it was corrupt; for all flesh had corrupted their way. (RSV)

THE CHRONOLOGY OF THE FLOOD

There were 40 days during which the rain fell (Gen. 7:12)	40 days
Throughout another 110 days the waters continued to rise, making 150 days in all for their 'prevailing' (Gen. 7:24)	110 days
The waters occupied 74 days in their 'going and decreasing' (AV margin). This was from the 17th of the seventh month to the 1st of the tenth month (Gen. 8:5). There being 30 days to a month at that time, the figures in days are 13 plus 30 plus 1	74 days
Fourty days elapsed before Noah sent out the raven (Gen. 8:6,7)	40 days
Seven days elapsed before Noah sent out the dove for the first time. (8:8) This period is necessary for reaching the total and is given by implication from the phrase 'other seven days' (Gen. 10)	7 days
Seven days passed before sending out the dove for the second time (Gen. 8:10)	7 days
Seven more days passed before the third sending of the dove (Gen. 8:12)	7 days
Up to this point 285 days are accounted for, but the next episode is dated the 1st of the first month in the 601st year. From the date in Genesis 7:11 to this point in Genesis 8:13 is a period of 314 days; therefore an interval of 29 days elapses.	29 days
From the removal of the covering of the ark to the very end of the experience was a further 57 days.	57 days
TOTAL	371 days

With acknowledgment to the New Bible Commentary IVF.

11 | Mystery of The Mammoths

The torrential volumes of ocean rushing over the heights would sweep along those huge whales, mammoths, rhinoceroses, hippopotamuses, all to be dashed into pieces. Fragments of teeth and fractured jaws and bits of skull of animals and man mixed up with the teeth of a lion or hyena have been found embedded in the hard breccia of caves. Here would be a massive elephant's tusk and there would be bits of horns and bones of dismembered beasts.

These all help us to imagine the tremendous sudden nature of the worldwide catastrophe and the great force and violence of the invasion of the continents. Near the north pole, great mammoths would be engulfed in freezing seas and quickly frozen solid in blocks of ice.

Scores of these have been found when the melting ice in Siberia has disgorged a whole woolly elephant thousands of years old preserved fresh in the ice with the grass it was eating still green in its mouth when it was suddenly overtaken by the freezing sea (See fig 10). An Oxford anthropologist told me he had attended a mammoth-steak dinner made from these deep frozen mammoths. He said the meat was delicious!

Pre-Flood Animals in America

In America, huge mammoths perish and horses, lions, tigers and other wild beasts and even camels are drowned right across the continent.

Fig 10 Mammoth from Beresovka, Siberia

▼ CHECKPOINTS ▼

WORLDWIDE EVIDENCE

1. Skeletal
Animal bones on mountain tops. Not syncline fossils.
Mammoths of Siberia frozen whole in ice blocks.
Mammoth bones frequently uncovered in USA.
Whales in Alabama (mid-continent) bones used for fences.
Pre-flood animals under stratum in USA (horses, lions, etc.)

2. USA Sites with Flood disjunction
Wildcat Cave (Dr D. Cole)
'Dirty Shame' site.
Fort Rock, Oregon.
Lake Titicaca in Andes agricultural ridges now frozen at 12,000 feet.

3. Calendar Changes after Flood
Greater angle made bigger seasonal contrasts (Gen. 8:22).
Only 360 days in year before Flood.
Reason for 360 degrees in circle and compass.

Ancient Calendars had 360 days and 12 months of 30, eg.:
Noah's Calendar. 5 months = 150 days to Flood peak (Gen. 7:11, 8:3, 4).
Hindu Calendar. 360 with 12 x 30 (Thibant's *Astonomie*).
Chinese Calendar. 360 with12 x 30 (per Medhurst).
Greek Calendar. The same (per Heroditus).
Babylon cuneiform script had 360. Same for Romans (Plutarch) and Incas of Peru and Mayas, Persia and Egypt (Total 10 nations).
Proves major planetry disturbance.

12 Sharing A Common Ancestry

Migration from Ararat to Iraq and Babel

'**N**ow the whole world had one language and a common speech. As men migrated from the east they found a plain in Shinar and settled there' (Gen. 11:1 NIV).

With the passing of years, the survivors of the Flood made their way along the Iranian mountain plateau south-eastwards. Some of them descended into the Indus valley towards the East, where their culture has been excavated at Harappi. Others descended westwards into the Mesopotamian valley. Here they are called Ubaidians, from their type site at al'Ubaid. In the totally different environment of Mesopotamia, they were forced to use new materials for the buildings and crafts.

The evidence supports the Bible by showing that the earth was repopulated from a common ancestry and from a common geographical area, from which we can trace the spread of mankind after the cultural hiatus of the Flood incident.

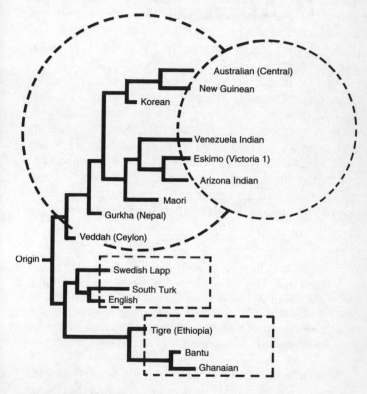

Fig 11 Racial family tree computed from blood group gene frequencies

Nimrod the Mighty Hunter

The latest sports news of the day 3,500BC makes a headline in Genesis 10:8. Featured large is the hero Nimrod—a name which has fascinated mankind ever since. He was one of those charismatic pioneers, not only of sport, but also in the founding and building of several city states. This was after the devastation of the Flood. What a list of achievements he had to his name, Nimrod.

First, consider his sport. His name was proverbial. 'Nimrod, the mightly hunter before the Lord.' In addition, he planned and built separate autonomous communities. They became known as city states. The planning was to avoid a centralised despotic empire. Each city state would have the local interests of the community at heart. The ruins of each city are, today, the prime interest of archaeologists and anthropologists. Genesis 10:8–12 is a running commentary upon their discoveries:

> And Cush begat Nimrod: he began to be a mighty one in the earth. He was a mighty hunter before the Lord; wherefore it is said: Even as Nimrod the mighty hunter before the Lord. And the beginning of his kingdom was Babel and Erech and Accad and Calneh, in the land of Shinar. Out of that land went forth Asshur, and builded Nineveh, and the city Rehoboth and Calah, And Resen between Nineveh and Calah: the same is a great city. (RSV)

The most famous of those city states is Babylon. This was called Babel at first. To my mind, the fact that things went wrong at Babylon centuries later is not the fault of Nimrod. Late in history, Babylon became all that is typical of false religion. Also ambitious despots forsook Nimrod's ideology of local government and created for the area an empire which was to impose its errors and rule all over the then known world.

CORRELATION OF GENESIS ARCHAEOLOGY AND CULTURE

1. **Before the Flood:** Genesis 2:8−6:13.
   Shanidar-Zarzi complex of caves, and earliest farming experiments 10,000BC
   First City-building Era:
   New Stone Age and Chalcolithic Catal Hüyük, Hacilar.
   Natufian and New Stone Age Jericho.
   North Mesopotamian villages of Hassuna and Halaf type.

2. **The Flood:** Genesis 6:14−9:17.
   Post diluvian dispersion, Genesis 9:18−10:32.

3. **After the Flood**
   Commencement of Second City-building Era in South Mesopotamia:

   ● Genesis 11:2
   Migration from Ararat along Iranian plateau (Zagros Mountains) south-eastwards, then descent from the east on to the flood-plain of Sumer (Shinar) of South Mesopotamia.
   Ubaidian colonisation of the marshes (c.3900BC); reed huts, irrigation; an important step forward. Some hundreds of years represented by the word 'settled' (RSV).

   ● Genesis 11:3
   Mud bricks appear first in the Ubaidian phase as there was no mountain-stone available on the mud flats. Even sickles and roof nails were made of baked clay. Warka phase follows.

   ● Genesis 11:4
   Protoliterate phase of city states with temples, 'Come let us build a city' (c. 3500BC)
   Ziggurat building commences with heaven-temples at the apex. A ziggurat was a man-made mountain reflecting the mountain origin of the immigrants. Writing commences 3400BC.

---

13 Tablets Tell Their Tale

▼ CHECKPOINTS ▼

FURTHER ILLUSTRATED BY RECENT DISCOVERY

1. Legal procedure
Hittite sale of cave and field to Abraham (Gen. 23) is on legal terms practiced in Abraham's time 1900BC (K.A. Kitchen, Liverpool University).

2. Contemporary practice
In the time of Jacob 1900BC, Rachel took the family 'doll' or teraphim. The reason would not be known even to Moses. Archaeology reveals that the possession of the teraphim meant a right to a father-in-law's property.

3. Literary style
Ugarit tablets 1400BC showed same style of poetry as in the Song of Miriam in Exodus 15.

4. Educational methods
Gezer calendar, 1000BC, is a schoolboy's exercise tablet. It gives the annual farming rotation, and reflects Old Testament scripts of David's time.

5. Parallel scripts
Samaritan Pentateuch (copies still exist) is found to be in the same style of script as the Siloam Inscription of Hezekiah's time, 721BC when the Samaritans were first taught the Torah.

6. Transmission accuracy

'The correct transmission of names is notoriously difficult'. Copies of Manetho's list of 140 Egyptian kings when compared with Egyptian monuments, has 63 of them unrecognisable in any single syllable. In contrast to this secular writer, 'the text in the Hebrew Bible has been transmitted with the most minute accuracy'. Dr J.W. Wenham, *Christ and the Bible*, T.P.

▼ CHECKPOINTS ▼

THE HUMAN AUTHORS OF THE OLD TESTAMENT

Time of Writing According to Evidences Given in the Manuscript

The Old Testament	Writer or Compiler	Date
The Pentateuch (Torah)	Written by Moses	14th—15th century BC
Joshua	Written by Phinehas, son of Aaron	c. 1380BC
Judges to the end of 2 Kings	Compiled by Jeremiah	c. 580BC (Note 1)
The Latter Prophets (Isaiah, onwards)	By the Prophets named	8th – 5th centuryBC
1 and 2 Chronicles to Esther	By Ezra and Nehemiah	5th centuryBC (Note 2)
Wisdom Literature	By those named	14th century to exile

Note 1. Jeremiah used the contemporary accounts of Samuel 'who wrote the manner of the kingdom' 1,000BC, Nathan, Gad, Ahijah, Iddo, Shemiah, Isaiah, and others of the School of the Prophets, and official royal court chronicles.

Note 2. They used the contemporary records of Shemiah and Iddo (2 Chron. 13:22), Isaiah (2 Chron. 26:22), Nathan, Ahijah and Iddo (2 Chron. 9:29).

Two Isaiah's?

Two of the books of the prophets most attacked are Isaiah and Daniel.

The second half of Isaiah's work was attributed to another writer later. In this way, the critics attempted to account for the fulfilment of the remarkable predictions of the emperor Cyprus. The critics did not believe that God could foretell and plan the future. Other critics even said there was a third Isaiah. But there are several clear indications of the unity of the whole book.

The Unity of Isaiah

First there are over 300 words and expressions common to both sections—the former and latter part of Isaiah. Moreover, the exile and return are not only written about in the second section but are also prophesied in the first section of Isaiah 11:11 onwards.(See also Isaiah's words to Hezekiah in 2 Kings 20:16–18.)

Second, there is a phrase quite peculiar to Isaiah which runs through the whole book and is equally distributed between the two supposed halves. (The chapters of the supposed first Isaiah are 1 to 39, and the supposed second Isaiah are chapters 40 to 66.) The phrase is 'The Holy One of Israel' and it refers to God. This occurs fourteen times in the first 39 chapters and sixteen times in the last 27 chapters, making a total of 30. The phrase occurs only six times in the rest of the Old Testament, and four of these are in that part of history, 2 Kings 19, for which Isaiah would be responsible. The other two are in Jeremiah, the compiler of that history. The phrase is certainly the Isaiah hallmark throughout his book.

THE TRUTH OF THE TORAH

The Torah

Scroll called Torah (Law) is Moses' work (Genesis to Deuteronomy). Called Pentateuch when translated into Greek 288 BC at Alexandria Meaning: five books. Was one scroll before division. Can see end and beginning of each was continuous originally.

So when in Deuteronomy 31:24, Moses finished writing the Torah, it was the **Pentateuch he placed in Ark for safety**.

Hilkiah re-discovered it in 731BC. 2 Chronicles 34:14−21

Wellhausen (1860) said Religion evolved. Not revealed to Moses as claimed.

So he reshuffled it (JEDP) and said was not completed until 400BC

Hittite legal code 14th centuryBC shows Pentateuch was by Moses. Critics still ignore this, and still cut up text according to God's names.

Anthropologists (eg. Professor Evans-Pritchard) and Archaeologists found Religion did not evolve.

Primitive belief in creator, but degenerated to animism.

Professor F.K. Kitchen finds ancient authors use two names for God 'Yaw' and 'El' in one text, eg. Ebla tablets, so JEDP theory is wrong.

Torah copied for Samaritan immigrants in 722BC.

So existed before 400BC. Their copy matches style of Hezekiah's conduit tablet 701BC.

Synagogues still keep their Torah scroll in an Ark cupboard, from Mosaic tradition.

Phinehas was Moses' Scribe.

Themes in the Torah are worked out in rest of Bible. Finalised in Revelation.

Sacred Scriptures

We know from experience that some whose faith has been strengthened by scientific evidence for the Bible have had that faith undermined later by a more subtle attack, criticism.

Paul Kanamori was a native of Japan. At school one of the boys found a Bible. he was fascinated as he read it, without the help of a missionary or a commentary. He was converted to Jesus Christ. He could not keep the good news to himself, and so he let other boys in his school read it. Many were converted, and without any adult teachers they formed themselves into a fellowship, until they numbered 100. Their ages ranged from thirteen to eighteen years.

The joy of salvation took them into the market place to proclaim their good news.

Kanamori gradually took the leadership, but they were severely persecuted, and Kanamori was cast into prison. He was searched but hid the gospels of Matthew and John in the inner lining of his waistcoat.

When he was released, he wanted to become a pastor, so he went to a theological college. He was taught all the theories of Higher Criticism, and sadly what persecution could not do, this subtle deception accomplished. He was taught that the Bible was only a collection of myths. God had not revealed his truth to the Old Testament prophets; religion had merely evolved; there was no creator; and the resurrection was all imagination.

He lost his faith and for 24 years he continued in the darkness of unbelief. Then tragedy struck. His greatly-loved wife died leaving him with his nine children. He was shattered.

Then into his thoughts came scriptures he had learnt long ago. 'I am the resurrection and the life, says the

Lord. He who believes on me, though he were dead, yet shall he live.'

He returned to the Saviour, and the old joy returned, and his eyes were opened to the clever deceptions which had tripped him up.

That same Higher Criticism is still taught today. It is compulsory for most of those who take preachers courses, so that is why you have had the opportunity of letting the Bible speak for itself.

▼ CHECKPOINTS ▼

THE BIBLE SPEAKS

1. The Former Prophets: Joshua to 2 Kings

- Phrase 'Unto this Day' indicates contemporary recording: Rahab rescued from Jericho 1400BC was still alive 'unto this day'. So book of Joshua was recorded by a contemporary writer, see also Judges 1:21.

- Jerusalem so famous after David's kingship was unknown when Judges was written. Judges 19:10.

- The contemporary writers from Samuel to 2 Chronicles are named six times. They were Samuel, Nathan, Gad and Ahijah, Iddo, Isaiah, etc.

- The Bible history is not the secular history which has perished (1 Kgs. 14:19) and which were the official court records, not Kings and Chronicles of our Bible. **Ezra named 22 writers of sacred history but knows nothing of supposed JEDP compilers.** Yet Ezra names everybody who did the least thing!

- Evidence that Jeremiah used these writers to compile Judges to 2 Kings. eg. 'Ears Tingle'. Phrases typical only of Jeremiah.

2. The Latter Prophets: Isaiah to Malachi

- Nearly all give date and reign of their prophecy, yet higher critics usually say it was someone else living hundreds of years later pretending it was a prophecy. Why? Because they did not believe that God could foretell the future.

- Yet this is what proves he is God according to Isaiah 46:9.

3. Isaiah

- It enables Isaiah to prophesy Cyrus and Exile 200 years later, but a second Isaiah is postulated by critics as writing after the event which detailed analysis disproves.

- Three hundred words common to all 66 chapters, and phrase peculiar to Isaiah. 'Holy One of Israel' occurs equally throughout. Therefore only one author.

4. Daniel

- He notes who reigned when he wrote from 588BC onwards, but critics say it was written after 165BC when a prophecy was fulfilled.

- Yet Daniel had already been translated into Greek by 288BC.

---

14 | Abraham's Army

Q *What was Abraham doing with a private army?*

Well, these tablets which have been found are called the Execration Texts. First they throw light on the meaning of a word in Genesis. It is 'Hanikim'. Men of influence had them. They were retainers or private soldiers. They would have regular inspections.

One tablet records an inspection of private armies which took place in the city of Ur, which was Abraham's city. This was in 2000BC—the time of Abraham. The tablet shows that others had small private armies too. It gives a list of them. The smallest was 40 soldiers and the largest was 600. So that means that Abraham's army of 318 was about average in size.

Archaeology has opened up a whole new vista of Abraham's culture.

Abraham would regard himself as a modern, educated man of his day. The idea that the Higher Critics had of Abraham as a primitive bedouin chief with a few sheep and goats nibbling at his tent pegs, has been changed by archaeological discovery. Thousands of tablets have now been deciphered which give us a very full picture of life 2000 yearsBC. We have more detailed knowledge of those times than we have even of medieval England!

Thirty thousand Accadian and Sumerian tablets descibe children's education, their mathematics, spelling tablets and work schedules, and nearly 2,000 children's 'text books' have been found in the form of tablets written by the children. History, religion and mathematics were taught.

Advanced systems of calculation included adding columns of sixty. This value column system made our modern calculators possible, and the figure 60 persists on our watches still, giving us 60 seconds to the minute and 60 minutes to the hour. The circle was 360°.

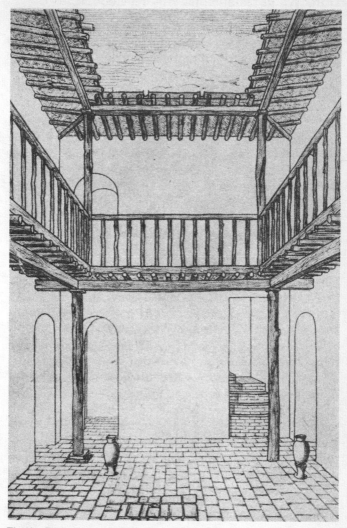

Fig 12 Restoration of a two storey house of the time of Abraham in the town of Ur 2000BC

► ABRAHAM'S ARMY

Donkeys versus 'Rolls-Royce' 2000BC

I have told you about Abraham's private army, to protect his transport business. What were these caravans like and how were supplies maintained?

The size, numbers and system are surprising. Dr Dent says, 'there are Syrian records of caravan trains with 3,000 donkeys! There was an elaborate maintenance system. Grass was planted along the trails to feed the pack animals. People were employed to made specially-terraced fields. They had to fetch water and lived in beehive-shaped houses along the routes. The caravan donkey was a particular breed. It could travel for two or three days without water while carrying a pack weighing 150–200 lbs. One man would control five donkeys and walk behind their charges, but the leader would ride on a donkey.'

Camels were also in use in Abraham's time. The Bible critics did not know this and their out-of-date accusations that the association of camels with Abraham was an anachronism—as has been portrayed on television—is wrong. Some theologians are still teaching it though.

Bones of domesticated camels 2000BC have now been found, but the camel was a prestige symbol, only ridden by the general manager. It was his 'Rolls-Royce'. When Abraham's steward journeyed north to 'Crossroads', to find a suitable bride for his master's son, Isaac, it was his master's 'Rolls-Royce' camels he took. He would only have donkeys for himself (Gen. 24:10). 'The servant took ten camels, of the camels of his master, and he departed.' (RSV)

'ROLLS-ROYCE CAMELS', 2000BC

1. **The Bible dates make harmony with history;** Some critics give dates 200 years later than Bible dates and then accuse Bible of not matching history.

2. **Tablets tally with truth:**
   Abraham's private army parade (Ur)
   Abraham's Business
   Abraham's Mortgage risk (Eliezer) Genesis 15:2
   Abraham's Family international transport company
   Four Kings versus five is an historical fact
   Deeds on The Doll for Rachel. Legal knowledge lost later
   Court cases at city gates.

3. **Camels were the 'Rolls-Royce' of the Bosses**
   Only donkeys for employees.

4. **Abraham's advanced civilisation 2000BC**
   Algebra and Arithmetic for Abram at Ur.
   The proof: 60 secs; 60 mins; 360 degrees on our watches and compasses, come from Ur.

The Ruins of Sodom and Gomorrah tell their Story

A convincing instance is the geological history of Sodom and Gomorrah, past, present and future. The first reference to Sodom comes early in Scripture. Turn to it in Genesis 10:19. It refers to Sodom and the cities of this Dead Sea valley as the area of prime beauty and productivity which was inhabited by the descendants of Noah's son Ham. In this verse there is no hint of the destruction to come in the days of Abraham. We can therefore reasonably conclude that the source of this information is prior even to Abraham himself.

City of the Dead Sea

Remember that the Lord punished Sodom for its homosexuality by making fire and sulphur rain down from the sky.

As I have said, if you go down to the Dead Sea, you can see the evidence for the destruction of that city of Sodom. If you walk round the southern end you can pick up lumps of sulphur even today, and the salt which rained down and engulfed Lot's wife can be seen around on the peaks and rocks. They are encrusted with salt!

There is a salt mountain with a 150 feet thick stratum of salt. The earthquake ruptured this and the fierce volcanic fire would melt it as it shot up into the air and rained down its terrible death upon those who disbelieved God's warning.

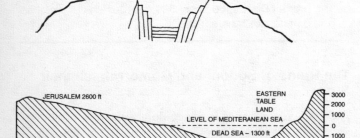

Fig 13 The cross-section of a typical rift valley and the rift of the Jordan valley to scale

You can also see the bitumen if you paddle in the Dead Sea at some spots. This tar, melted by volcanic heat, rained down all aflame.

Sodom and the Jordan valley were at the northern end of that great rift valley which runs south down into Africa. In that same rift valley in Africa, there are lakes of tar. A lot of our motoring roads are made from it.

The extraordinary experience of this rift valley is featured throughout times, in Ezekiel, and to the last days in Revelation. God knows beforehand when these geological events are going to happen!

First we have a description of its beauty long before Moses. Where did this information come from? Perhaps it was handed down from Abraham. Archaeology has found evidence which confirms that the area was extremely fertile before the overthrow of Sodom and Gomorrah. Beneath the barren sterile soft soils of the surface there is a thick layer of rich soil.

15 | God, The Geologist

Another example of God's 'incidental geology' is in Isaiah 40:12 where God says he 'weighed the mountains in scales and the hills in a balance' (NIV). This is called 'isostacy'. The height of the hills and mountains is counterbalanced by the depth of the 'root' of the elevated area. The 'root' goes down deeper into the sima of the plastic crust and remains balanced by its weight.

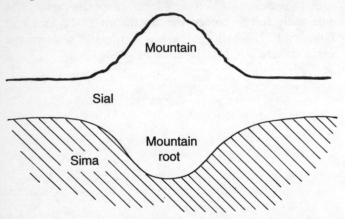

Fig 14 An example of Isostacy in which the upthrust of a mountain is counter-balanced by a 'root' protruding into the sima

We have already seen that the Bible indicates that life is created by God's words, the DNA code, and how Psalm 139 refers to the genetic book of Man. We have also read God's explanation to Job (chapter 38) of what makes the sun rise, namely the earth turning on an axis described in the Bible as like a Babylonian clay cylinder on a spindle.

▼ CHECKPOINTS ▼

GOD THE GEOLOGIST: useful list of proofs

1. God gives correct order of events.
   Supported from Astrophysics and fossils.

2. God tells three prophets of rift valley events to come (Joel, Ezekiel and Zechariah).

3. God tells Job that the earth turns on an axis and hangs on nothing (Job 38:12–14).

4. How God made valleys into mountains (Is. 40)
   - by weathering (v.4)
   - by synclines
   - Isostasy 'Mountains in balance' (v.12).

5. Jesus knew that at his second coming in parts of the world it would be night, morning, afternoon [knowledge of Earth globe] (Lk. 17: 34–36; Matt. 24:39–42 KJV)

6. Jesus knew nuclear fission would come through uranium. So did Peter [elements] (2 Pet. 3:12).

7. Paul was told that the resurrection body was an atomic change 'in atom' (1 Cor. 15:52).

8. Quantam physics 'By him all things hold together' (Col. 1:17).

9. Visible things were created by 99% invisible according to quantum mechanics (Heb. 11:3).

Moses Vindicated

One of the things that one critic said in his TV series, was that there was no evidence that Israel came out of Egypt in the year 1250BC. That's the event that we call The Exodus. He said that the whole story is fictioned. It never happened.

Of course it didn't. Not in 1250BC anyway. You see, the Bible says it happened 200 years earlier. If people don't take the Bible's dates to guide them, they are bound to get things wrong. The Bible says it took place in 1440BC. If you accept the Bible date, you will find that all the events of Exodus in the Bible slot into the framework of Egyptian history marvellously.

This is the kind of circular argument which is typical of the sceptics. They manufacture their own contradictions and then accuse the Bible of them.

Q   *Where in the Bible does it say that the Exodus happened in 1440BC?*

There are two or three places describing the Exodus; 1 Kings 6:1 is one place where it says that Solomon started to build the Temple 480 years after the Israelites escaped from Egypt. The date of Solomon's Temple was 960BC 'even sceptics agree with that date'. Add 480 to 960BC and that gives you the date of the Exodus as 1440 BC. Now if those critics started with the Bible date, they would find that Egyptian history not only fits in, it explains why Moses ran away from Egypt at the age of 40, why he returned 40 years later, who the Pharaohs were, and the archaeology slots into the whole framework. The whole list of dates and events in the Bible harmonises perfectly.

CRITICS DEBATE

1. Three TV programmes ignore information and biblical alignment:

Bible	Egyptian Archaeology
Joseph	Foreign Shepherd Kings
Slavery	Nationals gain throne 18th Dynasty
Moses Adopted	By Princess Hatshepsut (Thotmes III)
Moses flees	Hatshepsut had died
Exodus	Amenhetep II
1st born death	Thotmes IV not the heir
Conquest 1400	Amenhetep III (Akhnaton) ignores appeals found on Amarna tablets

2. Three days journey to Hatshepsut's temple for Moses
Moses Hebrew name 'Manasseh' inscribed
'Drawn out' is meaning of 'Moses' on tablet

3. Hasty entombment of Amenhetep II
Sphinx slab by Thotmes IV testimony (after Exodus)
critics wrong reckoning
'You are idle' on Egyptian mural (cf. Ex. 5:17)

4. Beetle symbol (Scarab) = Egypt (British Museum)
Reduces Patestine resistance to Israel's conquest
(Ex. 23:28; Deut. 7:20 'Hornet')

5. Amenhetep III brings monotheism to Egypt (cf. above)

6. Experts in Archaeology reject lack of knowledge of Higher Critics

Fig 15 Evidence of the Hebrew slaves in Eygpt

GOD, THE GEOLOGIST ◀

16 The Impact of Israel

T he critic adds that there are no monuments either in Egypt or Palestine that refer to Israel. But this in not correct. It should be realised that none of the Egyptian monuments ever refer to a defeat. Consequently, the escape of the slaves is sarcastically recorded as the 'escape of lepers'. Moreover, the entry into Palestine is recorded on the Tel Amarna tables. The Caananites had been appealing for help from the Pharaoh Akhnaton. The tables ask for help to stop the Israelite invasion. They say that if he doesn't, the whole of the land will be overrun.

A Desperate Plea for Help
Here it is—a loyal soldier called Abdkhiba writes about Jerusalem to Egypt. He wrote to this Pharaoh Akhnaton:

> 'The king's whole land will be lost. Behold the territory of Seir as far as Carmel, its princes are wholly lost and hostility prevails against me.' He has appealed apparently several times for he goes on, 'If no troops come this year, the whole territory of my Lord the king will perish.' Then he appeals that the king will at least send forces to ensure the retreat of himself and his men doesn't happen and in a postscript he adds to Akhnaton's secretary, 'Bring these words plainly before my lord the king. The whole land of my lord the King is going to ruin.'

The tablets say that the Hebrews were invading from

Seir and Edom and the Bible says that that is where the Israelites launched their invasion. You find the details in Deuteronomy 2.

Q *Did Pharaoh Akhnaton actually send his army to help the Caananites?*

No, he didn't, and there is a good reason why he didn't. He knew now that the Pharaohs could not fight against God. The ten plagues and the crossing of the Red Sea and the miraculous drying up of the River Jordan had proved that.

The Lamb and Lintel

The tenth plague, however—the death of the first-born—has no natural explanation. God moved in a token judgement against sin, fearfully demonstrating what the wages of sin are. For all who would believe and obey, there was a graciously provided means of escape— the Passover. In every household there would be one death—either that of the firstborn, or that of the divinely-appointed substitute lamb.

Q *Why were both lamb and lintel needed to deliver Israel from Egypt?*

Look at the lamb first. In how many ways did the lamb foreshadow Christ? First, God said the lamb must be perfect. It must have no blemishes. This depicted Jesus who was without sin, or blemish. That is why he could die in the sinner's place.

Second, the lamb must be slain. So the Lord Jesus was killed for us. His blood atoned for our sins, 'Behold the

Lamb of God which takes away the sin of the world', said John the Baptist.

Was the lintel also necessary? You know that a lintel is the top of a door frame.

Israel was not delivered from Egypt because of their nationality. They were delivered because they applied blood to the lintel. God said that anyone who did not apply the blood, was to die when the angel of death passed over the land. If an Israelite did not apply the blood of the sacrificed lamb, he died whatever his nationality. Also, any Egyptian who applied the blood would be saved. In fact, there was a mixed host who came out of Egypt with the Israelites. So you see, it was the lamb and the lintel. It was not sufficient for the lamb to be slain, the person had to spread the precious blood onto the lintel post of the door of his house.

The Crossing of the Jordan

On one occasion when I was going along the Jordan valley, I took a photo of the place where the river Jordan got blocked off. Jordan ceased to flow when steep soft banks collapsed, just as Joshua reported.

Just think about that for a moment. It shows God's control over natural events. God was actually telling Joshua before it happened that the banks would collapse just at the right moment, just as the ark of the covenant was approaching the flood waters. The waters would shrink away just at the speed with which the priests marched forwards with the ark.

As I stood there, I imagined Joshua also standing there and writing in his report those words in chapter 3:16:

'The waters which came down from above stood and rose up upon a heap not far from the city called Adam, that is beside Zaretan, and those waters which came down toward the Dead Sea were cut off.'

Did you know that the same thing happened in 1927. Sir Charles Marston tells you in his book, *The Bible Comes Alive,* that an earthquake shook Palestine in 1927. This made those soft banks collapse as they did in Joshua's day. This made Jordan dry up for 22 hours. Such a length of time would give ample time for the armies of Israel to cross over and camp at Gilgal, ready to attack Jericho.

S.O.S.

Archaeology has revealed something not recorded in scripture. The alarmed kings in Canaan sent urgent requests for help to Pharaoh of Egypt. Their letters or tables were found in his record office. As we saw, they are called 'the Tel el Amarna Tablets'. They were found by an old peasant woman in Egypt when she was rummaging in the ruins. They are dated between 1400 and 1360BC. That time fits in perfectly. The Israelites are called Hebrews, but pronounced 'Habiru'. Notice that Pharaoh knows them as Hebrews in Exodus 7:16.

Here are some of the cries asking for Pharaoh's help:
1. 'The land of Shechem has gone over to the Hebrews'.
   Shechem was where Joshua read out the blessings and cursings from Deuteronomy as God instructed.
2. Another extract from the king of Sidon reads: 'Behold all my cities which the Pharaoh has given into my hands have fallen into the hands of the Hebrews.'
3. Another king (of Gebal) wrote: 'He has conquered

beyond the land of the Amonites. The city of Sidon
has submitted to the occupation of his allies. The
lands are for this Hebrew, so now there is none
who is a friend to me.'

▼ CHECKPOINTS ▼

MIRACLE TIME

1. Three main miracle periods—Exodus, Elijah, Emanuel

2. Ten Plagues. Ten years natural calamities happen together
in months (but 'first-born' fatalities were supernatural)
Sphinx slab evidence to Pharaoh's first-born fatality

3. The God of Nature:
Red Sea recession by gale (Ex. 14:21)
Jordan dammed up by soft soil slip (Josh. 3:13–16)
Happened again in 1927—Jordan blocked for 22 hours

4. Jericho's mound and 'The spy who loved me'
Amarna tablets plea for help 1400BC
Tablets ignored—Pharaoh frightened of Jehovah
Canaanites cruelty to children
Rahab ancestress to the Redeemer (Matt. 1:5)

---

17 | The Long Day Substantiated

Heroditus, the great historian of ancient times, tells you that the priests of Egypt showed him in their records the existence of an unusually long day.

There are six independent records by ancient nations of this long day. The Indian Hindu account says, 'In the life of Chrishnu, the sun delayed setting to hear the pious ejaculations of Akroon; that planet went down to make a difference of about twelve hours'. The date? It corresponds with Joshua's date (about 1400BC)!

Professor Totten has stated that research shows that a whole day of 24 hours has been inserted into the world's history. Professor Totten has found that the sun and moon have only been in that juxtaposition once. I quote,

> '...by taking the equinoxes, eclipses and transits, and working backwards to the winter solstice of Joshua's day, it is found to fall on Wednesday, whereas by calculating forwards to the winter solstice of Joshua's day, it is found to fall on a Tuesday. So a whole day of 24 hours has been inserted into the world's history.'

So Professor Totten affirms that 'not before or since has there been a date which will harmonise with the required relative positions of the sun, moon and earth as conditioned in the Holy Scripture'.

The Superintendent of Greenwich Observatory noted, from Joshua 10:12–13, that the sun was at midday and the moon at the horizon—the valley—north-west at Aijalon. With this astronomical information, he was able to project back and find that it happened on the 21st July.

E.W. Maunder, Fellow of the Royal Astronomical Society, late of the Royal Observatory Greenwich, wrote about the subject and traces not only the actual spot on which Joshua must have been standing at the time, but the date and time of the day when this remarkable phenomenon took place. Does the Bible give so much detail? Yes! Joshua 10:12 says, 'Sun, stand thou still at Gibeon, and thou moon, over the valley of Aijalon.' You see, the Bible is so accurate that it tells you the actual position of the sun and moon in the sky at the time.

The scripture says that the sun stood still for about a whole day, so that would mean nearly 24 hours. Astonomers find that a day has been added to the astonomical calendar. The final 40 minutes or so (10 degrees) would be that added as a sign to Hezekiah, in 2 Kings 20:10.

JOSHUA'S LONG DAY

He said, 'Sun, stand thou still over Gibeon and thou moon over the valley of Aijalon.'

They obeyed and the sun stopped in mid-sky for nearly a whole day. How's that for a Guinness Book of Records entry? As a matter of fact, it was recorded in the Guinness Book of Records of that day. It was called the 'Book of Jasher'.

Reasons for the Long Day

Enemy rushing to city safety
Joshua not equipped for seige warfare
Jasher, The Guiness Record book of ancient times
Joshua 10:13; 2 Samuel 1:18

Records of Long Day

Heroditus 500BC and Egyptian records
Indian Chrishnu account
Other ancient records—China, Aboriginal, American Indians
Professor Totten's equinoxes, eclipses and transits
Superintendent of Greenwich Observatory. 21st July
Position moon and sun. Joshua 10:12
E.W. Maunder Royal Astronomical Society

How?

Sir Ambrose Fleming and 'Krypton Factor'
Comet influence and meteorites

Other Notes

Rahab was still alive when Joshua was written (Phinehas, Moses' Secretary)

Table of Time

1400BC   Bible date for the Long Day
300 Years to Jeptha (Judges 11:26)
180 Years Jeptha to Solomon from (1 Kgs. 6:1)

18 | Tablets and Temple

Tablets found actually describe the transport of timbers from King Hiram to the Temple of Solomon. Hiram was a Phoenician and these records were written by a man named Sanchuniathon. He says that King Hiram transported timbers and planks on 8,000 camels.

Q *But hang on a minute, Victor. A critic said that camels weren't in use until 360 years later than this.*

This tablet proves this theory is true and critics wrong, doesn't it? Think of it! Eight thousand camels to transport cedars to the Temple building project. Now listen to the equivalent account in the Bible. It's in 1 Kings 5:6: 'Solomon said, instruct the cedars of Lebanon be cut for me for no one among us knows how to cut timber like you people of Tyre.' Hiram replied 'I'm ready to do all that you desire in the matter of cedar and cyprus timber.'

Q *But what do the tablets add to the information in the Bible?*

It gives the actual names of those mariners. There were Kedorus, Jaminus and Kotilus. It also says that Hiram sent highly skilled bronze workers to Solomon's Temple. One such worker is mentioned here in 1 Kings 7:13, I quote, 'He was the son of a widow of the tribe of Naphtali and his father was a man of Tyre, a worker in bronze, very skilful for bronze work. He came to King Solomon and did all his work.' (RSV)

The Ras Shamra tablets from the coast of Syria are poems and psalms about David's time and of course the wisdom of Solomon was famous for his proverbs and natural history. Solomon was a great expert on horses. He imported horses from a place which the Bible calls 'Que'. We've only learnt recently that this was a place away in Asia Minor (Turkey). This was where the famous horse culture of the Hittites arose. They took to breeding white horses. One white horse was worth four times as much as an Egyptian horse. You can imagine Solomon riding a great white horse.

▼ CHECKPOINTS ▼

SOLOMON'S EMPIRE

1. **Two critics say there is no evidence of Solomon's buildings. The reason:**
   'Not one stone left' at Jerusalem's prophesied fall in AD70 but Solomon's casemate style visible at:
       Gezer, Hazor, Megiddo Forts (A Millard, Liv. Univ.)
   Phoenician materials (2 Chron. 2) confirmed

2. **Camel blunder by critic said not used until 601BC**
   Corrected by experts:
   - Professor Zeuner—camels domesticated in Abraham's time 2,000BC
   - Sanchuniathon says Solomon's transport had 8,000 camels! He confirms all the details of 1 Kings 5:8–11
   - Professor Kitchen lists evidence 2,000—1,400BC

3. **Ingots from India**
   - Confirmed by Jerome and Greek Septuagint

4. **Critics should take 'tablets' to correct scepticism:**
   - Hiram of Tyre confirms temple materials
   - Hiram sent experienced sailors
   - David's psalms style on Ras Shamra tablets

- Solomon's horses from 'Que' Turkey (Ras Shamra tablets)
- Solomon's stables unearthed at Gezer, Hazor, Megiddo
- Bible lists cities Israel failed to capture

▼ CHECKPOINTS ▼

Joshua to Solomon

A. 300 Years from the Conquest to Jephta's first year

West of Jordan	No. of yrs	East of Jordan	No. of yrs
Joshua and Elders	20		
Mesopotamian oppression	8		
Rest (Othniel)—Judges 3:11	40		
Moabite oppression—Judges 3:14	18		
Ehud and Shamgar—Judges 3:28 to 4:1	80		
Sisera's oppression—Judges 4:3	20		
Deborah and Barak—Judges 5:1,31	40		
Midianite oppression—Judges 6:1	7		
Gideon—Judges 8:28	40		
Abimelech—Judges 9:22	3		
Jair's era—Judges 10:3	22		
Tola of Ephraim—Judges 10:2	23		
Ammonite invasion of West Jordan after 18 years in East Jordan—Judges 10:9	1	Ammonite oppression in East Jordan ending with the invasion of West Jordan	18
Jephta's total—Judges 11:26 TOTAL	300	since 2½ tribes entered East Jordan	

The problem now is in accounting for the remaining 180 years between Jephta and Solomon, to bring the total to 480 years (1 Kings 6:1). There are two factors to note, the first is that the Philistine oppression runs concurrently with Samson and Eli Judgeship. This is clear from Judges 13:1; 15:11, 20 and 16:31. The second is that the duration of Saul's reign is unknown in the Old Testament record. The 180 years work out thus:

B. 180 Years between Jephta and Solomon

Jephta—Judges 12:7	5	
Ibzan of Bethlehem—Judges 12:9	7	
Elon—Judges 12:11	10	
Abdon—Judges 12:14	8	
Samson—Judges 15:20; 16:31	20	Note 1
Eli—1 Samuel 4:18	40	
Samuel—1 Samuel 7:2; 14:18	20	Note 2
Saul (by deduction	27	Note 3
David—2 Samuel 5:4,5	40	Note 4
Solomon to 4th year—1 Kings 6:1	3	
TOTAL	180	
Plus 300 to Jephta	300	
GRAND TOTAL	480	

(1 Kings 6:1)

Note 1. Philistine oppression of 40 years runs concurrently with Samson and part of Eli's judgeship;
Note 2. Unlikely to be longer as he was a boy in Eli's 40 years and did not die until the end of Saul's reign.
Note 3. At Saul's death, David and Jonathan were about 30 years old (2 Samuel 5:4,5) therefore were teenagers together fifteen years earlier when Saul had reigned twelve years. Jonathan would be about three years old when Saul was crowned (say at the age of 23 years—married at 19).
Note 4. Saul would be 50 when slain: men usually ceased to go into battle after 50 years of age.

TABLETS AND TEMPLE ◀

19 | The Falkland's Jonah

There are on record three or four cases of seamen who have been swallowed by a whale and have survived. One was an Arab who fortunately had his sharp dagger with him. With this he cut a way out of the stomach and escaped.

The best known case is the Falkland's Jonah. His name was James Bartley and he was swallowed by a whale, but survived to tell his story.

He was a member of a whaling crew on the ship 'Star of the East'. The crew sighted a spout of water coming out of the sea and knew it was from a whale. They gave chase and when they were near enough, fired a harpoon. In the effort, Bartley fell overboard and, in spite of a search, he was nowhere to be seen. Eventually, after half a day trying to get the poor whale on board, they managed to haul it up and land it on the deck. By this time it was dead.

They cut open the stomach and out fell James Bartley, unconscious.

They threw a bucket of sea-water over him to restore his consciousness. When he came round he was raving mad, His skin had been parched to a deadly white by the gastric juices of the whale.

He had been in the whale's stomach for nearly a day. When he recovered sanity, he said that inside the whale he had plenty of air but it was very hot. He fainted from fear, not from lack of air. The whale was of the cachalot species which has no grill in its mouth and is able to swallow even sharks. It often vomits up contents of its stomach onto the shore, just as Jonah was vomited up.

Jonah thought God could not bring him back from a paid-up passenger spot in the sun on a cruise to sunny Spain. But that is where he underestimated God's natural resources. God had already created an air-conditioned submarine sea mammal. Jonah was going to have a whale of a time learning to pray down on the ocean floor, 'I cried to you out of the belly of hell!' Dear me, Jonah, what language!

Fig 16 Ancient Tarshish: Jonah's escape route in the ancient world Tarbessos or Tarshish was near Gibralter, which was a port of call on the way to Brittany (Oestrimnides). A stop would also be made at Marseille (Massilia)

Dr Layard finds Ninevah

But the usual doubters doubted the story of Jonah, not only about the whale, but also what the Bible said of the size of this immense city. It was three days journey in breadth. This was nearly 800BC and was about 100 miles NNW of Baghdad. Dr Layard was a Higher Critic at first. He accepted without question all that criticsm asserted. He believed that the story of Jonah was only a myth with a moral. Archaeology had hardly started to correct corrupting concepts. Then Dr Layard made an expedition to ancient Nineveh and excavated its ruins. The public were astonished when he wrote his famous book *Nineveh and its Remains*. He found that Nineveh was all that the Bible said it was. I quote Jonah 3:3:

> 'Nineveh was an exceedingly great city, three days jour-
> ney in breadth and Jonah began to go into the city, going
> a day's journey, and he shouted, "In 40 days time Nine-
> veh will be destroyed by God." '

On page 336 of his book, Layard says concerning the extent of the city, 'The dimensions of the city were 150 stadia for the two longest sides of the quadrangle, and 90 for the shortest, the square being 480 stadia or almost 60 miles...The three days journey of Jonah should corres-pond exactly with 60 miles of the square formed by the great ruins...20 miles in a day's journey in the East, and we have therefore exactly three days' journey'.

Layard found that Nineveh was indeed a 'mighty city'. Its walls were huge like Babylon's. The inner wall was 76 feet high and 32 feet thick. That is wide enough for four traffic lanes—the motorway of ancient times, like an M25 around the outskirts. It provided the possi-bility for chariot races upon the walls. 1,500 towers 200

Fig 17 Fish God Nina

feet high dominated the whole complex at regular intervals.

Bas relief sculptures on the walls show what a powerful culture it was—soldiers and chariots, shields and projectiles. But what is this low relief on the wall—**a man looking out of the mouth of a fish**—could it be Jonah? Who knows.

Can you swallow Jonah?

If ever there was a book in the Bible which was unlikely to be true, it is the book of the Prophet Jonah. Yet all its impossibilities have now been proved factual. Here is that list:

1. Jonah was swallowed by a whale and was coughed up alive
2. That Jonah paid a passenger fare for a sea trip as far as Gibraltar
3. That God had created a sea mammal able to swallow Jonah and keep him alive
4. That Nineveh was an exceeding huge city of 60 miles across ('3 days journey')
5. That the ruling despot noted for cruelty wouldn't take any notice of Jonah's threat of God's judgement
6. That God had a plant which could grow up in one night and wither away the next morning
7. That Jehovah God was a God of love who wants

to spare the children and cattle of cruel foreigners

Some have even questioned whether Jonah existed: 2 Kings 14:25 states clearly that he did. 'God spoke by the hand of his servant Jonah', in the reign of the northern Israel king Jeroboam II. He was contemporary with Hosea about 765BC.

Can you swallow Jonah? I thank God for my scientific training, for it is precisely because of it that I can reaffirm the truth of Jonah and the Bible.

▼ CHECKPOINTS ▼

JONAH—USEFUL POINTS

1. Cachelot whales can and have swallowed a man, eg. James Bartley
   Mystery of when and why whale was created
   Jonah's parched appearance would frighten superstitous tyrant

2. Passenger sea trips featured in ancient times
   Pictures on Nineveh's walls

3. Sceptics doubted Nineveh's size until Layard excavated it (60 miles diameter)
   Walls 76 feet high, 32 feet thick

4. Palmcrist Plant does grow and whither rapidly as in the Biblical record

5. God revealed his love in Old Testament very early, eg. Exodus 20:6 (cf. Jonah 4:2); 1 Kings 21:25–29; Psalm 18:6,18; Jeremiah 9:23,24; Lamentations 3:23; Hosea 2:20

---

20 | The Great Crises

Dr Dent comments, 'It may have been in the plain between the Tower of Babylon and the Palace of Nebuchadnezzar that the 'image of gold' was set up. This statue was 100 feet high and 10 feet wide and was a representation of himself which was to be worshipped. Records tell us that Nebuchadnezzar made public use of worshipping statues not only in Babylon , but also in Ur.

When the three Hebrew children refused to bow down to this image, they were punished by being thrown into a fiery furnace. Excavators at Babylon have found a furnace with the inscription, 'This is the place of burning where men who blasphemed the gods of Chaldea die by fire'. Also, a ruined college library was discovered revealing curricula for native princes. They were instructed and trained especially for 'Interpretations of dreams and visions'. 'Impiety to any gods—cast alive into a fiery furnace' and 'Untoward acts relative to a king—cast alive into the den of lions'.

For centuries the site of Babylon has lain waste. Critics thought that the Bible's description was a myth until archaeology revealed an amazing metropolis. Dr Dent sums up the archaeologist's discoveries:

> 'In the days of Nebuchadnezzar, the city of Babylon was large and grand. The walls were 60 miles in circumference, 80 feet thick and 300 feet high and its foundations went down 35 feet. Around its walls were 250 towers used as guard rooms. Surrounding the city was a moat and in the wall were 100 gates of brass. The city was

divided almost in half by the river Euphrates and 25 gates connecting streets with ferry boats. Over the river was a bridge with stone piers half a mile long and 30 feet wide. At night drawbridges were removed. A feat of ancient engineering was the tunnel which went under the river and was 15 feet wide and 12 feet high. The walls were so wide that chariot races were a common occurence and it is claimed that four chariots in line would race around the city on the wall.'

▼ CHECKPOINTS ▼

GREAT CRISES

1. The Elijah Crisis (answered by special miracles)
Jezebel replacing Jehovah by Baal horrors
Baal's castle at Mt. Carmel 'carved by fire' (Dr Dent)
Elijah challenges 850 there. Shows fire comes from Jehovah
Water in Drought: twelve barrels poured over sacrifice!
Palestine government survey reveals artesian basin with three and a half years supply; outlets at Carmel and Beersheba

2. The Daniel Crisis
Ten days test passed with credit
Feet of clay image prophesied 2,500 years of history
Evidence for furnace furore
Inscription 'This is the place of burning'
Penalty for impiety—cast alive in furnace fire
Training curricula for native princes (Dr Dent)
Area cleared for mass worship (Leo Woolley)

3. Babylon
Historical record and writing on the wall
City fell 16th October 539BC
Repeated in 1988 to Ayatollah—glowing cross

Daniel third in kingdom. Discovered that Belshazzar was
vice-regent
Critics thought Babylon a myth
Digs confirm. Walls 80 feet wide, 300 feet high
250 towers, 100 gates of brass
Impressive main entrance

4. The Book of Daniel
Critics wrong on Aramaic, but still ignore discoveries
Aramaic spoken 200 years before Daniel (Dan. 8–12 in
Aramaic)
Daniel wrote 588BC but critics date it 165BC because of
unbelief in prophecy
Greek translation made 100 years before critics date!

*Now available! The Book which reveals exciting
new evidence for the reliability of the Bible.*

Archaeology

Archaeology *will enable you to:*

☐ **Answer doubts of the reliability and accuracy of the
Bible raised by critics**
☐ **Explore archaeological discoveries in the light of
biblical history**
☐ **Understand the true chronology of events recorded
in the Bible** *plus much more*

Evidence For Truth: Archaeology 320 pages. Illustrated with
black and white photographs and diagrams throughout. Can
be obtained   from good Christian bookshops. In case of
difficulty contact:
Alpha Books, Raans Road, Amersham, HP6 6JQ Tel: 0494 722151

21 Why Question The Virgin Birth?

Why is scripture so outspoken about the necessity of the virgin birth? Only the God-man could be a sufficient payment for sin or substitute for sinners like you and me—we who have done wrong in God's sight. It was essential for your salvation and mine. That is why the angel told Joseph to name him Jesus which means Saviour, because he will save his people from their sins (Matt. 1:21).

> The cross and the virgin birth are immediately tied together here. One cannot be effective without the other.

But what is the real reason why some question the virgin birth? It is because they do not believe in miracles. The Lord said beware of the yeast of deception of the sadducees. He warned us that such unbelief would come into the church later.

Now we are clearly told in Acts 23:8 what kind of unbelief this is. The Sadducean religion did not believe in miracles.

Modern genetics reveal that the pairs of genes (alleles) from both parents make one person at conception. The statement 'That which is conceived in her is of the Holy Spirit', shows how God was the Father and the virgin Mary the mother. Also, the fact that DNA is a code demonstrates how the speech, or 'Word' of God, recorded upon the nucleic acids, would form the real genetic contribution from the Divine side. We see how that Christ was fully and truly man, and yet not two natures, but God-man, not God and man, thus illustrating physically what had been arrived at theologically by earlier divines.

Yet ultimately our only authoritative source for the doctrine of the Incarnation is still the revelation of God in Holy Scripture.

▼ CHECKPOINTS ▼

VIRGIN CONCEPTION

1. **A sacred subject,** but we must meet the critics' objections.
   In the creation of Eve from Adam's cell, the 'Y' chromosome would be removed.
   With the Virgin, it would be added by the Holy Spirit (Lk. 1:31–35)
   Verse 31 says it was a conception, therefore not parthenogenesis.
   Holy Spirit would supply or recode DNA for the word made flesh. Alleles (genetic pairs) from the two sources, human and divine, would become pheno, typically one, for one personality not two natures.
   'With God nothing shall be impossible' (v.37)
   St. John 1:1–14 applies Genesis 1:1—5

2. **Near East Marriage customs**
   Engagement could not be dissolved without a divorce.
   Consummation not allowed until marriage.
   This made possible the Virgin conception, then marriage and Christ's virgin birth within wedlock

3. **Kindred tablets of descent**
   Both from the same ancestor by different routes
   Mary also had a kindred link with a priestly line (Zechariah)

For Jesus to be born in Bethlehem, Joseph must also be descended from David.

4. **Salvation** could only be accomplished by a God/Man.

The DNA Code and the Incarnation

The scriptures persist that the Word which coded in the beginning became recoded in the virgin Mary at the Incarnation by similar agencies as those at the beginning.

The prologue to the fourth gospel is a striking application of the phraseology of Genesis 1. It becomes very much more arresting today as we are able to reconsider it in the light of our knowledge of genetic coding. 'The Word' of John 1, known to the Greeks as the Logos, is an application of the repeated expression of Genesis, 'God said'. This is emphasised by other analogies which John makes. The passage is among the best known of the Bible:

> In the beginning was the Word
> And the Word was with God,
> And the Word was God.
> The same was in the beginning with God.
> All things were made through him,
> And without him was not anything made that was made.

The prologue concludes with a statement demonstrating to us that this same 'Word' who himself coded all life in the beginning, graciously allowed himself to become coded in the DNA of the Incarnation:

> And the Word became flesh, and dwelt among us,
> And we beheld his glory,
> The glory as of the only begotten of the Father,
> Full of grace and truth.

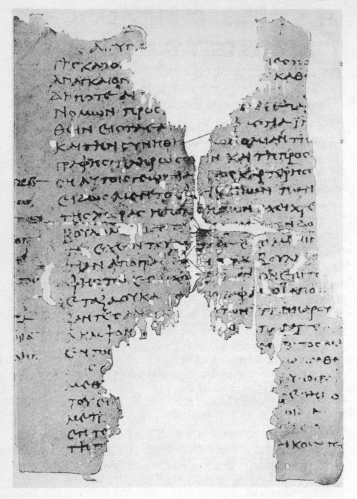

Fig.18 Census of Caesar. An example of an edict 2,000 years old, commanding everyone to return to their native town similar to the one recorded by Luke 2:1–6 which led to Jesus being born at Bethlehem.

WHY QUESTION THE VIRGIN BIRTH? ◄

22 | More Historical Than Anybody

I continue to get letters or see in newspapers the assertion that the picture of Jesus in the New Testament is not a factual one. This is often backed up with the assertion that there is little in history about the man Jesus Christ.

Such statements are completely without foundation. They only deceive people who have no knowledge of the facts.

The New Testament story of the Lord Jesus has three times more evidence of its accuracy than any figure of history; three times more than anything about any of the Roman emperors; and many times more written copies of the original accounts. Compared with any event of history, the New Testament has abundantly more reliable documents that any.

Professor F.F. Bruce of Manchester University, says that Caesar's Gallic War with which many students are familiar, has only nine old copies and the oldest of those is 900 years after Caesar's day, yet nobody questions those. In contrast, the New Testament has 5,000 Greek manuscripts of the New Testament in whole or part. The oldest full copies go back to about AD330 and part of St. John's gospel which has survived, actually goes back to within a few years of St. John's original writing, and we have fragments of St. Mark's gospel and St. James' letter and 1 Timothy older than AD68.

Of the works of the Roman historian Livy of Christ's time, only twenty old copies survive. What a contrast to the 5,000 of the New Testament. The well-known Roman historian, Tacitus, has only four surviving old copies of his Annals. What a contrast to the 5,000 old manuscripts of the New Testament.

Concerning the famous history by Herodotus, the oldest copy of the original is 1,300 years later than when it was written. Professor Bruce comments, 'Yet no classical scholar would listen to an argument that the authenticity of Herodotus was in doubt.'

He then reviews the wealth of evidence we have for the New Testament and shows what a contrast it is to secular history.

▼ CHECKPOINTS ▼

THE REAL JESUS

1. **Motive** of critics is to say that Jesus was only a prophet, who, in the second century, the Church exaggerated into a miracle-working Messiah
   Reason: they thought miracles impossible

2. **Pilate** was said to be fiction, but:
   Memorial stone found at Caesarea Barracks
   Tacitus Roman historian AD115 'Executed by sentence of Pontius Pilate, in reign of Tiberius'

3. **Jesus more historical than anybody:**
   Three times more evidence than any other historical figure
   Caesar's Gallic Wars has only nine copies no older than 900 years
   New Testament has 5,000 Greek manuscripts. Oldest fragment is AD68
   Tacitus has only four old copies
   Heroditus history—oldest copy of original is 1,300 years later

4. First century historians refer to Christ:

Eight non-Christians (Tacitus, Suetonious, Serapian, Phlegon, Lucian and Josephus, as well as references by Pliny and Thallus)

Nine antagonists (Talmuds)

Four gospels: Eyewitnesses, 'accurately' Luke 1:1

Quotations from Apostolic Fathers AD86—108 from all the New Testament

5. Examples:

Josephus—fairly full concise summary of Christ

Pliny—in a sacrament Christians 'worship Jesus as a God'.

Thallus—three hour darkness reached Rome

Serapion—Fall of Jerusalem because Jews executed Jesus

Talmuds—'Hanged him on Eve of Passover'. 'Illegitimate'

23 | Bulletin: A Strange Inquest

Lawyers' Inquest

Seven high ranking lawyers have given their verdict. An unusual feature was that the body was missing. Search parties reported that a man had been seen walking seven miles on badly torn and wounded feet.

Three of these lawyers received such reports with *great scepticism*. Their names were Gilbert West, Lord Littleton and Frank Morison. After intensive detective investigation they reached an amazing conclusion. The other four also used their long legal expertise to thoroughly sift such fantastic claims.

The claims were that the missing body had actually chatted with hundreds of people for nearly six weeks all around the country! Had he been really dead? The chief executioner, on solemn oath, said he had thrust a spear right through the victim's heart which entirely emptied itself in blood and serum. All the other witnesses were called, and the unanimous verdict by all these leading lawyers was that this man had actually risen from the dead!

The findings of the last four were as follows:

Sir Edward Clark, KC: 'Evidence is conclusive'
Lord Lyndhurst: 'Such evidence has never broken down.'
Simon Greenleaf (the great authority on legal procedure): 'No possible motive for fabrication.'

Professor Anderson: 'Empty tomb stands—a veritable rock of evidence.'

▼ CHECKPOINTS ▼

LAWYER'S INQUEST

1. **Three Lawyers** set out to prove Jesus did not rise:
   Frank Morison, *Who Moved the Stone?*
   Gilbert West and Lord Littleton, both Rationalists.
   Examined evidence by legal methods
   It proved the Resurrection. They set out the evidence.

2. **Two eminent Christian lawyers** give their legal findings:
   Professor Norman Anderson, 'Empty tomb stands, a veritable rock of evidence.'
   Sir Edward Clark K.C. 'Evidence is Conclusive'.
   Lord Lyndhurst, 'Such Evidence has never broken down'.
   Simon Greenleaf, 'No possible motive for fabrication'.

3. **Dr John Stott** examines the mystery of the empty, hollow, mummy-like grave wrappings. They made John believe when he saw them.

4. **Prophesied in Old Testament**
   Psalm 16:8–11; Psalm 22; Psalm 110:1; Psalm 118:22–24; Job 19:25; Isaiah 53:10

5. **Jesus predicted** his death and resurrection over seven times:
   Matthew 12:38; 16:21; 17:9; 17:22; 20:18; 26:32; John 2:18.
   But they could not understand it.

6. **When he had risen** (Lk. 24:45)
   'He opened their understanding that they might understand the scriptures, and he said to them, "Thus it is written and thus it behoved Christ to suffer, and to rise from the dead the third day".'

The Resurrection Jigsaw Puzzle

What excitement and confusion on that first day of the resurrection! There was running about, reporting the empty tomb, seeing angels, seeing Jesus. All this was mixed with incredulity turning into amazed belief. In the confusion of reports coming in, it was not easy to sort out the order of events.

All the accounts from the four gospels and Paul's list in 1 Corinthians 15, are like a jigsaw puzzle. I have found it fascinating to put the pieces together—and I want to tell you this—yes they all fit! Yes, there is harmony in the accounts.

There are sixteen jigsaw pieces to the complete picture. They are sixteen accounts of twelve incidents. It is because some have reduced the pieces to only half the number that they could not fit them together.

A Packed Refresher Course
Thirty-nine days were to follow in which Jesus appeared and disappeared—five-and-a-half weeks in which they never knew when he might appear again, when he would appear to give them further instructions and insights into the scriptures and an understanding of the purposes of God for the world. Nearly six weeks in which their own hearts were to be examined, in which they were to see their weaknesses and be prepared for the Lord's new miraculous strength.

RESURRECTION JIGSAW PUZZLE

Fitting in twelve appearances of the Risen Jesus.

1. Jesus appeared five times on the First Resurrection Day

Two women saw the stone rolled away, Mary Magdalene and Mary, James' mother. 'Men will only think it's a tale.' Told no one, only 'Body is missing'.

- Mary stays and sees Jesus
- Mary catches up with former Mary and both see Jesus
- Christ's personal interview with guilty Peter
- Two walking to Emmaus. Tell apostles who exclaim, 'He's appeared to Peter'.
- Sunday evening to all in upper room. They had been prepared by reports. 'I'm not a ghost!' Old Testament foretold it all

2. Next 39 days, another seven times

(A packed refresher course on Old Testament prophesies)

- Next Sunday in the upper room to all, especially Thomas
- At Galilee lakeside as reminded by the angel. Seven disciples including John 22
- On a mountain in Galilee to all eleven apostles. Recommissioning, including Matthew 28:16
- One hundred and twenty including Holy Family and holy women in upper room, Acts 1
- Five hundred Brethren in one gathering
- Then to James, half-brother of Jesus. (Christ's origin needed explaining)
- The Ascension from Mount of Olives with promise to return

24 The Dead Sea Scrolls

Unfortunately, the media is often ready to seize on statements by a sensationalist if they knock the Church or the Bible.

There have been several instances of this concerning the Dead Sea scrolls. It has given the public the impression that they expose Christianity as something invented by those who wrote the scrolls from 130BC to AD68 and they go on to accuse the Church of trying to cover up these things. The accusation is laughable for anyone who knows even a few basic facts. The scrolls actually are a great testimony to the accuracy of our Bible text.

Instead of there being an attempt to prevent the scrolls coming to public attention, it was prominent clerics and scholars of the church who rescued many copies and bought them so that they could be translated for all to read.

No Cover-up

Five of the scrolls were found in Cave one. The Archbishop of the Syrian Orthodox monastry in Jerusalem, bought them and as he could not read Hebrew, he told the American School of Oriental Research about the find, hoping that their scholars could translate the scrolls, so there was no cover-up there.

By the Lord's providence, John Trevor was director and a good photographer. he photographed each column of the great scroll of Isaiah. This was 24 feet long and ten inches high. In great excitement, he sent some of the prints to Dr W.F. Albright in USA.

Albright replied immediately.

'My heartiest congratulations on the greatest manuscript discovery of modern times...What an incredible find! And there can happily not be the slightest doubt in the world about the genuineness of the manuscript...I date it around 100BC.' He meant that it was about the year that this copy was made from earlier copies. These in turn went back to when Isaiah wrote the original during a period around 740 to 722BC.

▼ CHECKPOINTS ▼

A COVER-UP?

1. **Not a cover-up** by the Church. Clerics and scholars rescued them, eg.:
   Syrian Orthodox Archbishop
   American Oriental School of Research
   John Trevor sent photo of Isaiah to Dr W.F. Albright
   Professor Sukevik bought three scrolls for University of Jerusalem the day State of Israel voted
   Yigel Yadin significance, son of Professor Sukenik
   Yigil Yadin quotes 'Assumption of Moses' which instructs scroll preservation. Also Jeremiah 32:14

   Eleven caves 200 manuscripts covering every book (not Esther)
   + Essene commentaries
   Essenes described by Origen AD185–254

2. **Cover-up was by sceptics**
   They misrepresented them before they had been read
   A critics dope accusation. Later challenged by Yadin, Vermes and Carpenter

Fourteen years later another critic confessed to sensational inaccuracy

Geza Vermes and Albright correct false statements of others as 'emotive' and say 'not affected Bible message'. Supported accuracy of copying

Millar Burrows agrees

Demolishes 'second' Isaiah theory. God proves he is God by foretelling Cyrus and Exile. Josephus agrees

Then, an Australian writer in 1992 probably misinterprets Hosea's experiences as reference to Christ

3. **Essenes** did not invent Christ, neither did Jesus get his ideas from them

They were quoting Old Testament prophecies describing Christ, eg.:

'The Son of Man' from Daniel 7:13

'Teacher of Righteousness' from Deuteronomy 18:15–19, etc.

'He is to judge the world and save elect and divide between sons of darkness and sons of light', from Daniel 12:2,10, and Joel, Isaiah, Ezekiel and Zechariah

'The New Covenant' from Jeremiah 31:31–34

The Scroll of Isaiah

Those of us who have seen the Isaiah scroll know that what is now chapter 39 in our Bible ends one line up from the bottom of the scroll column. The next line at the very bottom starts what is now our chapter 40, which some thought should be by a different author, but obviously if another author was writing, a fresh column would have been started.

As I have said, it demolishes the theory of two Isaiahs. If you look at the photo of the end of our chapter 39, you will see that it ends one line up from the bottom and what we now call chapter 40 starts on the

Fig 19 Scroll of Isaiah

bottom line and continues onto the next column. There is obviously no concept of an ending and starting of a new work by someone else.

The critics denied that it could be one work as early as 722BC because they did not believe that there was a God who could reveal his future plans. They quote those passages in Isaiah which speak of Judah's return from Babylon through the help from Cyrus the Persian Emperor.

▶ THE DEAD SEA SCROLLS

121

USEFUL LIST OF EVIDENCE

1. Scrolls prove the accuracy with which our scriptures have been copied and handed down. They were copied for over a thousand years without an intervening copy surviving until the Dead Sea scrolls were found.

2. They support claims of the Massorete method to ensure accurate copying.

3. Sir Frederick Kenyon, former Director of the British Museum, says that Bible copies are three times more reliable that the secular classics such as Shakespeare, Marlowe, or Greek and Roman history which nobody bothers to question.

4. A fragment of St. James' epistle was found in cave seven. This must have been copied from James' original some years before the jars were sealed in AD68, this gave the fragment from Mark's gospel.

5. The scrolls support the assertion that Isaiah was written by the **one** prophet Isaiah in about 740BC, showing that God **did** foretell his future plans. 'I am God and there is no-one else…declaring the end from the beginning, and from ancient times the things that are not yet done…I will fulfil all my purpose' Isaiah 46:9–10).

6. The scrolls got their anticipation of Christian phrases from the prophecies of the Old Testament:
   - 'New Covenant' from Jeremiah 31:31, 500 years earlier;
   - 'Son of Man' from Daniel 7:13 about 500 years earlier;
   - The 'Righteous Teacher' who would judge the world from Deuteronomy 18:15–19 (1400 BC) and Isaiah 42:1–4 (750 BC) and other prophecies
   - 'Bread and Wine'—Genesis 14:18 and Psalm 110:4.

7. The three sections of Old Testament scripture are summed up as complete, just as Jesus did in Luke 24:44, ie. The Torah, The Prophets and the Psalms, which all foretold the Messiah Jesus.

25 | The Ominous Year of AD66

Cestius surrounded Jerusalem for five days and his troops battered at the walls. Even the Christians in the city were apprehensive. Had not Luke recorded the words of Jesus years earlier, thirteen years ago in AD53? It warned the Christians to evacuate Jerusalem when armies surrounded it. (Matthew and Mark had not recorded the bit about the armies.) What did it mean? How could they escape if armies were all around the walls?

The deep valleys around the east, south and west of Jerusalem made the walls impossible to attack, so Cestius attacked from the north. The Christians wondered even more how they could obey Christ and escape.

Josephus then adds these significant words: 'He (General Cestius) retired from the city, without any reason in the world.'

But there was a reason! Can you guess it? Jesus had prophesied to the believers, 'When you see Jerusalem surrounded by armies, then know that its destruction is near. Then let those who are in Judea fly to the mountains, and let those who are inside the city depart, and let not those who are out in the country enter the city.' This particular warning was only recorded by Luke.

Josephus says, 'The Jews, after they had beaten General Cestius, were greatly encouraged by their unexpected success.' But he says, 'After this calamity had befallen General Cestius, many of the most eminent of the Jews swam away from the city as if from a ship when it was going to sink.' Who were these people?

It is Hegessippus, another historian, who tells us that those who forsook the city were the Christians. They read an oracle left by Christ. Now what oracle was that? It was recorded only in Luke's gospel. Here is evidence that Luke wrote well before AD66. Indeed, Luke's gospel had been written thirteen years earlier.

▼ CHECKPOINTS ▼

JOSEPHUS' HISTORY

1. **Jewish non-Christian** wrote history for Romans as observer.
   His record showed how Christ's prophecies were fulfilled AD66—70.
   High Priest Ananias executed James when Festus died.
   Festus also features in Acts 25 and 26.
   King Agrippa and Queen Bernice in Acts also figure in history.
   Florus slew 3,600 Jewish worshippers to steal treasure: this sparked revolt.
   Mob massacred Roman garrison and took their war machines.

2. **Cestius** surrounded Jerusalem in AD66. Josephus said certain ones fled.
   Luke recorded this thirteen years earlier (21:20,21) as the sign to flee whole country.
   Jesus knew this would start three-and-a-half years war over the whole land.
   Bethsaida, Chorazim, Capernaum would suffer. 'Woe unto you', wrote Capernaum's converted tax collector, Matthew 24:20.

3. **Vespasian and Titus** in winter of AD69 prepare attack on Jerusalem.
   'Pray that your flight be not in Winter.'
   Campaign postponed. Nero had died.
   Rebels, Zealots, and Temple guard renewed in-fighting.

4. **Titus** marched up as Passover approached.
   Sacrilege committed by Zealots warned remaining Christians.
   Jesus had wept 'Your enemies will make a bank and hem you in.'
   Three million Jews were trapped.
   Sacrifices ceased for ever as Daniel 9:27 prophesied.
   None necessary after Christ's sacrifice, Hebrews 10:1–22.

5. **'Captives into all nations'** Luke 21:24.
   Titus sent best young men for march of triumph. Now depicted on Rome's ancient Arch of Triumph with the branched lampstand of Exodus 25.
   Seventeen-year-olds sent in chains to Egyptian mines.
   Under seventeen-year-olds sold as slaves around the empire.

6. **'Until Gentile rule ends in Jerusalem'** Luke 21.
   It ended in 1967 with Israel back in Jerusalem city.

Acts Vindicated by Archaeology

Sir William Ramsay was one who started by assuming that Acts was written too late to be accurate, but his archaeological discoveries and his knowledge of Roman history compelled him to revise his opinion. This was partly because the detailed descriptions and titles of the officials Paul met in various provinces were completely accurate. This knowledge of Luke must have been contemporary with the events because the titles of the provincial governors changed suddenly at times if the status of provinces changed. Yet Luke always uses the correct title of which there are about eleven occurrences.

Clues to Dates of Writing

Professor F.F. Bruce of Manchester University has pointed out that a clue to the date of the completion of St. Luke's Gospel is the date of the end of Acts which is a sequel to it. It is obvious that Acts ends unfinished. It was written up-to-date. Paul was a prisoner in Rome awaiting trial before Nero. If it was written after that trial in AD62, Luke would surely have recorded it. We can safely conclude then, that Acts was written before AD62 and Luke's Gospel a reasonable time before that.

What testimony have we to Matthew and Mark? A Christian writing as early as AD100 was a disciple of St. John. His name is Papias, and concerning Mark's Gospel, Papias says that Mark was Peter's companion and 'wrote down accurately all that Peter mentioned, whether sayings or doings of Christ...for he paid attention to this one thing, not to omit anything that he heard, nor to include any false statements.'

Of Matthew's Gospel, Papias said, 'Matthew compiled the sayings in the Hebrew Aramaic tongue (the language of Jesus) and everyone translated them as best he could.' Now it is significant that it is in Matthew's Gospel that we have the longest sections of 'sayings'.

I have given you evidence to help your faith in God's remarkable book. Paul wrote, 'We overthrow all reasonings and every proud thing that exalts itself against the knowledge of God and take captive every **theory** to the obedience of Christ' 2 Corinthians 10:5.

In the first Bible I bought after my conversion, I wrote in the flyleaf (prophetically?):

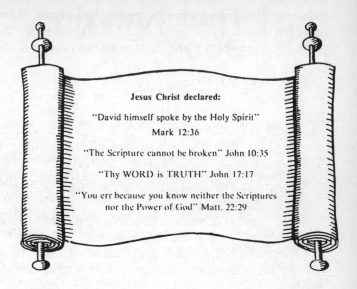

Jesus Christ declared:

"David himself spoke by the Holy Spirit"
Mark 12:36

"The Scripture cannot be broken" John 10:35

"Thy WORD is TRUTH" John 17:17

"You err because you know neither the Scriptures
nor the Power of God" Matt. 22:29

Fig 20 Scroll

'We've travelled together, my Bible and I,
Through all kinds of weather, with smile and with sigh.
In sorrow or sunshine, in tempest or calm,
Thy friendship unchanging, my lamp and my psalm.

So now who shall part us, my Bible and I,
Shall 'isms' or 'schisms' or 'new lights', who try?
Shall shadow or substance, or stone for good bread,
Supplant thy sound wisdom, give folly instead?

Oh no, my dear Bible, exponent of light,
Thou sword of the Spirit, put error to flight.
And still through life's journey, until my last sigh,
We'll travel together, my Bible and I.

(author unknown)

26 | That Amazing Book

The Bible is the most remarkable book in the world, looked at from any angle. It is the oldest book in the world. It has survived down 40 centuries of human history. Other ancient records have perished and have only been discovered by archaeology, but the Bible as a book has been handed down the ages.

Why is this? It is because believers were told by God that its records were to lead to the Saviour of the World, that it must be preserved and handed down from Abraham to the Apostles and from Adam to the second Adam.

The first section of holy scripture was the Torah of Moses from Genesis to Deuteronomy, then to this, God gave the prophets ever-increasing information to add. When the prophesied picture of the precious Saviour was complete in the Old Testament, the world waited 400 years until, 'In the fulfilment of time, God sent his Son'.

The living witnesses of Christ then wrote the New Testament. The canon of scripture closed when the last witness died.

Because holy and honest men were inspired by the Holy Spirit, (to use St. Peter's words), those records were accurate and affirmed by many infallible proofs, (to use Luke's words).

First Among Nations
The Bible is remarkable because it has been the first book to be put into writing for a high percentage of

nations, and has been the foundation of their civilisation. When it has been neglected or disbelieved, that country has declined, as God said it would.

▼ CHECKPOINTS ▼

THAT AMAZING BOOK

1. **Oldest Book in the world:**
   4,000 years to Abraham; 3,400 years to Moses.
   Why? To prepare for Saviour (Gen. 12).
   Prophecy ceased 400BC to wait for Saviour.
   Other countries' histories discovered only by archaeology.
2. **Miraculous preservation:**
   Attempts to destroy it and Christians.
   John for 'Word of God' on Isle of Patmos.
   Rome until 4th century. Traitors.
   Medieval church because it exposed added errors.
   More subtle Rationalists by Criticism infiltrating the churches.
   Satan says prophecies are fraudulent but Satan is the big fraud.
   (Jn. 8:44, Rev. 12:9)
3. **Says how God inspired the prophets.**
   • By audible dictation (not by divination forbidden Lev. 19:31; Deut. 18:10–20).
     Moses: audibly and face to face. (Num.12). 'I speak to Moses mouth to mouth and visibly'. Two-thirds of Exodus, Leviticus and Numbers are written down as dictated.
     Isaiah: 'I heard the voice of the Lord'
     Ezekiel: 'Hear with your ears'
     Daniel: 'He talked with me'. 'I heard but did not understand'.
     (So it was not his own ideas).
   • By vision usually with voice.
   • Told to write it down.
     Isaiah 8:1 'Write on a tablet and note in a book'.

Jeremiah 36:2 'Write all the words I have spoken in a book'. (RSV)
Ezekiel 24:2,3,14 'Write...I the Lord have spoken it. It will come to pass'.
Habakkuk 2:2,3 'Write the vision, make it plain'. (RSV)

4. For all time:

'Heaven and earth will pass away but my words will never pass away', said Jesus in all synoptics (Mk. 13:31).
'Your Word is forever' Psalm 119 'Endures for ever' 1 Peter.
'Not one comma (yod) will fail' said Jesus. 'Any teacher teaching it will be called least' Matthew 5:18,19.

5. Scriptures claim:

'All scripture is given by inspiration of God' 2 Timothy 3:16.
'Holy men spake as they were borne along by the Spirit of God' 2 Peter 1.
'David spoke by the Holy Spirit', said Jesus, Mark 12:36.
'The scripture cannot be broken' John 10:35
'Thy Word is truth' John 17:17.
'Anyone adding or taking away from this book will have his place in the Holy City removed', said God, Revelation 22:19.

Tax

As a trained tax collector of Rome, Matthew would continue his customary habit of taking down notes in the vernacular 'of all that Jesus began to do and to teach'. According to the Early Fathers, this was in Aramaic, the very language Jesus used.

Normally, when making tax reports, Matthew would then translate his notes into Greek and send them to Rome. It would, therefore be natural for him to translate his own notes taken during Christ's ministry into Greek after Pentecost when 'this gospel was to be preached in all the world' (Matt. 26:13).

The Early Fathers date it eight or ten years after the

resurrection. This would be during the expansion beyond Samaria into the Greek world; Matthew would see the necessity as indicated in Matthew 28:19,20, 'Go therefore and make disciples in all nations...teaching them to observe all things whatever I gave to you in command.'

Shorthand

It comes as a surprise to learn from Roman records that Matthew would be taking it all down in shorthand—a tax collector's shorthand script, then he would rewrite it in the vernacular (Aramaic), then translate it into a Greek report to Rome. Is that why we get the fullest records of Christ's brilliant preaching from Matthew?

Rome had a very elaborate and detailed tax system so that no one would escape. There were 111 categories of tax. As a tax collector Levi (an appropriate name before he became a disciple) would have full particulars—long before he became Matthew—of every household.

▼ CHECKPOINTS ▼

THE BIBLE SPEAKS
Testimony of Early Church writers AD70–170.

1. **Matthew** AD30. Aramaic notes during ministry. Papias b. AD70
   Aramaic underlies Greek translation—Bruce, Chilton, Howard
   Note taking prevalent in Christ's time
   'Certain Matthew passages more original than Mark's' (Blomberg)

2. **Mark** St. Peter's. Probably written in Rome AD44 after Peter's escape, Acts 12

'Wrote down accurately...paid attention not to include any false statement' Papias b. AD70

3. Luke AD54 or 57. William Ramsey's archaeological research finds Luke very accurate. Luke gives his methods:
- Information obtained from eyewitnesses
- Complete understanding from the first
- Wrote an order of events
- Others he knew had written their experiences
- Infallible proofs of Christ's life and miracles

4. Acts Completed AD62 before Nero outcome was known, therefore Luke earlier, probably AD54 (2 Cor. 8:18) or during Paul's first imprisonment AD57
Cf. Acts 21:8,9

5. John says:
- He was eyewitness (19:35)
- Confirms truth and accuracy
- Closest companion to Jesus (21:20–24)
- Gospel supplementary to Synoptics but before 'Wars of Jews'

Therefore AD65 (J. Robinson)

6. Other:
Significance of prophecy of Fall of Jerusalem
Warnings useless if written afterwards
Luke warned of armies surrounding Jerusalem AD66
Matthew and Mark warned of Fall in AD70
James, half brother of Jesus, very significant as Josephus refers to him.

27 | The Preplanned Destiny of Life

In comparing religions the question is often asked, 'What is special about Jesus?' The most effective reply is that which Jesus himself used and became the method adopted by the disciples afterwards. He showed that God had foretold and prepared for Jesus Christ for at least 2,000 years before he came. No other founder of a religion claims this. The prophesied details of his first coming are amazing, and all fulfilled.

What of his prophesied second coming? Are we to take that seriously?

This is a relevant question because in many circles it has become the fashion to avoid recognising the signs. Various excuses are given. Some have burnt their fingers they say, yet concerning other important doctrines there have always been people who lacked wisdom in their statements yet the scripture teaching has not been abandoned on those issues.

What did Jesus mean when he said, 'When you see these things coming to pass, then know that my coming is near'. Did he intend that Christians living near that time should recognise the signs, and perhaps have extra means of doing so?

Some Christians have found that the wise application of these signs has been an effective means of arousing the interest of the indifferent. Many statements by Christ show that he intended us to recognise and use the signs unfolding all about us.

You can see why some false teaching makes some

Christians weak in their witness to a sceptical world. Concerning science, the Old Testament is treated as a book of myths; concerning archaeology, the student is fed on wrong dating—not the Bible dates; concerning prophecy, he is told that the New Testament church expected Christ to return in their own life time. Consequently, such students see no remarkable creator's knowledge displayed in the Bible; they dismiss the harmony between archaeological tablets and Bible history, and see no significance in the signs of Christ's near return which are happening all around us.

I have given you convincing evidence to use from Science and the Bible in Volume 1; also amazing archaeological correlation which confronts the critics in Volume 2; so now we ask what are those prophetic signs, and are there indications in scripture that Christ knew that his return would be after a long time?

In answer to that last question, I bring to your notice areas of information which have long been neglected and even forgotten.

The evidence of prophecy, however, not only concerns Christ's second coming, it also establishes the claims of Christ made at his first coming. This is the effective answer to those who contend that Christ was only one of many prophets and only one founder among other religions.

Concerning scriptures which show that the period between the two comings would be a long one, a brief summary first will help you to see the relevance of the actual signs of his coming.

Briefly, God's time schedule in a number of scriptures says that Israel's scattering among the nations would last 2,500 years. This is revealed to Moses, Hosea, Daniel and Peter. The re-establishment of Israel on the map of Palestine after this period is a prelude to Christ's return.

Old faithful scholars' works on this have been neglected. Also, Christ gave many indications that his return would be after a long period of time. The evidence for all this was be given later but, after having voiced those points, the signs are then seen to be absolutely relevant. I outline the signs for your use.

28 | Effective Evidence

Whom are we to believe? Was Jesus Christ all that he claims to be? Is he just one among other founders of religion?

Prophecies in the Old Testament are an effective insight. No other founder of religion was foretold in the way that God prepared the world for the first coming of Jesus Christ 2,000 years ago. Every aspect of Christ's birth, life, atoning death and resurrection were described to the prophets hundreds of years before he came. From 2,000 *before* Christ, the full identity and credentials of the Messiah were described.

In order to help you master these, I give you full coverage for your own effectiveness. It was Christ's methods and it became the apostles' methods to demonstrate that Christ was in all the Old Testament scriptures.

There are also just as many prophecies describing his second coming and the signs which would show that it was near. These are effective in revealing to friends that the Bible message is relevant. Indeed, as you study the information you will find that *it is an amazing eye-opener* to the significance of what is happening in the world today. It is very topical and easy to converse about. Many an indifferent person has been sparked to eager desire for more insight. People generally are not aware of the amazing details in those prophesies. It is extraordinary how even commentaries on the Bible seem to miss the thrust of many a book of the prophets. Why is this?

I shall bring out all such evidence for your use. Without understanding this, the church is weakened in making its message relevant and convincing.

▼ CHECKPOINTS ▼

PROPHETIC EVIDENCE

Two Benefits of Evidence from Prophecy
1. For Christ's first coming it proves his claims, prophesied by many prophets.
2. For Christ's second coming, it is topical and makes the Bible relevant for non-Christians today. They see that events prophesied are daily world news.

Fashionable falacies which blunt perception
1. *That disciples expected Christ's return in their lifetime.* **Reply:**
a) They were intended so that their hopes were kept alive.
b) **Enigmatic Metaphors** intended to keep expectancy alive.
   - eg. Mark 9:1–2 says they will not die until the Kingdom comes with power. Next verse shows the Transfiguration as a fulfilment and Luke 9:28 connects the two. Power came to the spiritual kingdom at Pentecost.
   - John 21:21–23. John corrects wrong impression in v.23.
c) **'Certain things'**. Jesus did not know actual date (Mk. 13:32) but he knew it would be after a long time: Matthew 24:4 'These things must first be fulfilled but the end is not yet…Gospel first to all nations'.
d) **What things?**
   - Fall of Jerusalem AD70, scattering of Jews (Lk. 21:24) rise of Mohamet (Matt. 24:24). The return of Israel after 2,520 years from 603BC.
   - Matthew 25:5. Coming delayed so the Church falls asleep (v.48). Luke 19:12 'Far country'
   - Two thousand year-days Hosea 5:15; 6:2; 2 Peter 3:8; 2 Thessalonians 2:3 falling away first.
   - 2,500 years to pass. See Checkpoint section, item c.

2. *That God abandoned Israel in favour of the Church.*
Reply:
Romans 11:24 Israel to be grafted back in. Leviticus 26:44, Jeremiah 33:24–26.
3. *That Israel's return refers to end of 70 years Exile.*
Reply:
From exile only 2 tribes returned (Ezra 2:1; 4:1). From the *diaspora* all tribes are to return (Is. 11:12; Ezek. 37:16–24; Hos. 1:10,11).

---

29 | Signs

A lady remarked to me, 'Isn't it tragic that we hear little about the second coming just now when the signs show that it is near?' Yes, there are so many unmistakable signs. It is an impressive list which is powerful for convincing the casual enquirer.

'When you see these signs,' said the Lord Jesus Christ, 'know that my return is near.'

So let us take the word 'signs' as an acrostic to use when discussing them with a friend.

S for Science; I for Israel; G for Gospel; N for Nations; S for Society.

Many scriptures speak of stress, vandalism, terrorism, lawlessness, and the increase of wickedness which would characterise "the last days". 2 Timothy 3:1–6 reads like a daily press report. In fact, when one man in prison heard the passage read out, he asked, 'What paper was that in?'

> 'In the last days there will come times of stress, for people will be lovers of self, lovers of money, proud, arrogant, blasphemous, disobedient to their parents, ungrateful, unholy, cruel, refusing reconciliation, slanderers, sexual libertines, fierce, haters of good, treacherous, reckless, swollen with conceit, lovers of pleasure rather than lovers of God, holding a form of religion but denying its power'. Avoid such people.

This prophecy then moves on to the feature of increased education which does not promote God's revealed truth.

> They will be for ever learning but can never arrive at the truth...opposing the truth, men of corrupt minds and counterfeit faith...evil imposters, from bad to worse, deceivers and being deceived...people will not endure sound teaching...teachers will turn it into myths.

Certainly this prophecy is relevant. It is this unbelief and perverting of the truth which is the cause of our social ills today. Young people are not given guidance from divine authority which promises. 'Do these things and you will prosper in a good and happy life'.

Social geography also illustrates another prophecy. Students learn that the first invention to make the boys visit the lasses in the farther village was the boneshaker bicycle, and then the motorcar for the select few. Now, aeroplanes carrying 400 at a time speed through the air all over the world.

'Science and travel shall greatly increase'. That is what God told Daniel in chapter 12:4. Every time you pass a travel shop, you can say to your friend 'Daniel 12:4!' Every time an airliner flies over your head, you can point up and say, 'Daniel 12:4'.

▼ CHECKPOINTS ▼

AN ACROSTIC

'When you see these signs, know that my return is near'

S for Science
  Knowledge of travel increased (Dan. 12:4)
  Ever learning but erroneous (2 Tim. 3:7)
  Strong delusion to believe evolution (2 Thess. 2:8–11)
  Air travel from afar (Isa. 60:8,9)
  As birds flying (Isa. 31:5)
  Nuclear Fission (Mk. 13:25; 2 Pet. 3:12)

I   for Israel
  The re-united ten and two tribes will return in the last days
  as Israel: Isaiah 11:10–16; Jeremiah 16:14–16
  After a long time without a country (Hosea 1:10,11; 3:4,5;
  Ezek. 37:20–28; Amos 9:9–15
  Moslem date 1335 = AD1917 (Joel 3:1,2; Dan. 12:11,12)
  Nailprints to convert Israel (Rom. 11:25,26; Zech. 12:10)

G   for Gospel
  All nations must hear as a witness (Matt. 24:14)
  The ionosphere is in mid-heaven for radio waves and
  gospel proclamation (Rev. 14:6)
  Mouth of unclean propaganda war by Satan (Rev. 16:13)
  Christian radio penetrates closed countries (Rom.
  10:17,18)

N   for Nations
  Old Roman Empire now European Sovereign States
  before Christ descends to rule: (Dan. 2:28–45; Rev.
  13:17,18)
  United Nations flag regulates Israel's return; gentile
  nations ruled Jerusalem until 1967 (Lk. 21:24,25; Isa.
  11:10–16)
  World Wars (Matt. 24:6,7)

  Natural Signs
  Increase in earthquakes, famines, diseases (Matt. 24:8)

S   for Society
  Stress, vandalism, terrorism, lawlessness (2 Tim. 3:1–6)
  Truth forsaken by teachers (2 Tim. 4:3,4)
  Occult dabbling increase (1 Tim. 4:1,2)
  Lawlessness (2 Thess. 2:7–9)
  Wickedness increases (Lk. 21:34–36; Dan. 12:10)
  Wickedness decreases love of truth (Matt. 24:9–13)
  Fears and phobias at societies unrest (Lk. 21:26–32)

Now mark the texts in your Bible so that you can use them
easily.

---

30 Christ's Claims

What religion are we to follow? What sect are we to believe? Which founder of religion is the right one? These are the questions confronting you today. There is one sure answer. It is this. Only Jesus Christ was prepared for by prophecies all down the centuries before he came. Only Jesus was prepared for by God. The Creator told all the prophets of his plans to send Jesus to be the Saviour of the world. As the centuries passed by, more and more information was told to holy men who wrote it down in the books of the Old Testament—all the details about the Messiah's divine origin, his virgin conception, his ministry, crucifixion, resurrection, ascension and second coming.

That is why the risen Christ was able to show to his astonished disciples that he was foretold in all the scriptures from Moses to Malachi. All those 39 books of the Old Testament spoke of Jesus Christ long before he came.

> 'Jesus said to them, "O foolish men, and slow of heart to believe all that the prophets have written...And beginning with Moses, and all the prophets, he showed to them in all the scriptures the things concerning himself".' (Lk. 24:25)

Later he reinforced this evidence to all the disciples:

> 'Everything written about me in the Torah of Moses, and the prophets and the psalms must be fulfilled. Then he

opened their minds to understand the scriptures and he said to them, "Thus it is written and thus it was necessary for Christ to suffer and rise from the dead the third day, and that repentance and forgiveness of sins should be preached in his name among all nations".'

The disciples and early Christians followed Christ's example of proving him from the prophets and it is your most effective tool as well. That is why we shall look at those prophecies together and find how astonishingly detailed those prophecies were of every aspect of the Lord.

▼ CHECKPOINTS ▼

OLD TESTAMENT PROPHECIES PROVE CHRIST'S CLAIMS

In all three sections of Old Testament Christ was described

ie. in Pentateuch, Prophets and Psalms (Lk. 24:25,44)

1. *'Moses wrote of Me*
   Unleavened Shewbread ie. sinless, Exodus 25:30 (2nd person of Trinity)
   Lamb without blemish (Lev. 23:12; 1 Pet. 1:18,19)
   A new covenant (Deut. 18:15–19)

2. *Prophets also wrote of Jesus*
   To be born in Bethlehem (Mic. 5:2)
   As refugee from Egypt (Hos. 11:1)
   Ministry to be launched from Galilee (Isa. 9:1,2)
   Christ's life, death, atonement and resurrection (Isa. 53)

3. *Psalms* eg. Psalm 22 'Pierced hands and feet' and gambling for garments, could not be referring to David. See also summaries later in this section.

Divinity Described 'From eternity' Mic. 5:2. Son given is part of Holy Trinity (Isa. 9:6; 7:14; cf Jn. 14:9)

Creating Word 'I am the first and the last' (Isa. 48:12; Rev. 1:11; 22:13) The Word, God said, Genesis 1, Psalm 33:6,9. 'In the beginning The Word' John 1:1

By Virgin Conception
   Genetically through mothers Eve to Mary. Mitochondrial DNA .
   Mother's only mentioned in David's Kings eg. 2 Kings 18:1
   Sonship, Divine Source: proud Father Psalm 2:7 'You are my son'.
   In Gospels, God speaks three times 'You are my beloved son'
   Matthew 22:42–46. Psalm 110 'Lord said to my Lord'
   Sonship's Human Source: Body prepared (Ps. 40:6–8; cf. Heb. 10:5).
   Branch of Royal Tree. Isaiah 6:13; 11:1; 53:2. Shoot out of root.
   Zechariah 3:8,9. Atones on one day. 6:12,13. Priest-King. (Mary's lineage had priest affinities as well as royal.)
   Hebrew word 'almah' Isaiah 7:14 means virgin as in Genesis 24:43 so does 'Parthenos' in the Greek OT translation and 2 Corinthians 11:2.
   The virgin birth will be long after the exile (Isa. 6:11–13; 7:8).
   Two Geno-type sources become phenotypically *one* person.

Year-day Prophecy

Concerning prophecy, there is a neglected area which is very effective in convincing the unconcerned. Many Christians do not even know about it. Yet God gave it as a special proof of truth for those living 'at the time of end' (Dan. 12:9,10). Neglected Bible-believing scholars were Dr Adam Clark, Dr Gratton-Guinness and Dr

Basil Atkinson. The witness of Christians would be greatly strengthened again by getting to know about their findings. It is called chronological prophecy.

God told Daniel that the believers living in the end times would understand something which was concealed even from Daniel. What is it which God wants us to know which is special for those living in the end times?

Daniel asked, 'When shall these things end?'. He asked about times and seasons. It wasn't good for him to know. We can see that it would have been discouraging for him to know that the glorious climax to God's plan was still 2,500 years off. So he is given a mysterious number and figures which he didn't understand. Those living in the last days will understand, God said. To Daniel it was sealed up, but in Revelation 22 it is *un*sealed for those living when the second coming of Christ is near. 'Behold I come quickly', said Jesus. 'Do not seal up the meaning of these words'.

If the Lord made special provision for us to understand, it is surely wrong to ignore what he intends for the believer today. This not to be avoided merely because some have misused these figures. Some foolishly predicted the date of the Lord's coming. Those who did were *dis*obedient to Christ's words. 'The day and the hour no-one knows', but observe the signs.

On p.146 you will see that chronological prophecy was given early in the Bible to Moses as well as late to Daniel.

A dominant feature throughout scripture is that God is the God of the ages and has pre-planned history. This important theme is neglected but is an important answer to questions on the present evils and purpose unfolding in history.

Agnosticism has invaded theology so that statements like Isaiah 46:9–11 are ignored.

'I am God, and there is non other...
declaring the end from the beginning
and from ancient times things not yet done...
I have purposed and I will do it.'

To give an insight into the breadth of God's plan, is the purpose of chronological prophecy. Not so much to give dates as to show eras such as 1,260 years and 2,500 years.

▼ CHECKPOINTS ▼

WORLD HISTORY FORETOLD

A **Messiah** to come through Isaac, Genesis 17, through Judah, Genesis 49:10, succeeding Moses, Deuteronomy 18:15, through David, 2 Samuel 7:16, through Zerubbabel, Zechariah 4:7, through Mary, Luke 3:27.

B **The order of events** given to Joel, Ezekiel, Daniel and Zechariah:
1) Israel will return in the latter days
2) When Israel is settled they will be invaded
3) The Lord will descend to judge the nations
4) The Lord will then rule over all the earth
Note the order of events. The New Testament agrees with this order, eg. Matthew 25:31,32; 1 Corinthians 15:23−28; Revelation 19−20.

C **Prophetic Time Span:** The seven Times or 2,500 years of dispersion of Israel among the nations. One Time = 360 Years.
1) 360 degrees come from Sumerian time unit of 360, Leviticus 26:18,21,24,28
2) Each day represents a year; Numbers 14:34, Ezekiel 4:6, Luke 13:32, 33, Daniel 9:26.
Therefore 360 x 7 = 2,520 years.
Daniel 12:6, 1,260 x 2 = 2,520
First capture of Jerusalem 603BC to AD1917 = 2,520 years.

3) In 1917 Balfour Declaration opened Palestine to Jews. 1917 was also Moslem year 1335, see Daniel 12:12 (Dr Gratton-Guinness calculated correctly 31 years before fulfilment).

Learn Numbers 14:21: 'Truly as I live, all the earth shall be filled with the Glory of The Lord.'

Jesus in the Psalms

I have mentioned a few prophecies of Jesus in the Psalms. They are so remarkable that they are worthy of a section on them alone.

'Christ' named

These prophecies are not so often studied, yet they are very significant indeed. Many of them were written by David about a thousand years before Christ fulfilled them. Listen to Christ's own opinion about them! He said in Matthew 22:43 that 'David was inspired by the Holy Spirit'. In Luke 24:44 he said that 'everything which had been written about him in the Psalms must be fulfilled'.

There are about ten Psalms which prophesy about the Lord Jesus and they give over thirty details about the birth, life, the cross, resurrection, ascension and eternal priesthood of Jesus. That is quite a lot of detail isn't it from a thousand years before they were fulfilled? The details are remarkable ones too.

The second Psalm starts us off. Its fulfilment is quoted in the New Testament letter to the Hebrews. Did you know that the name of Christ appears first in this Psalm? The word 'Christ' is the Greek word for 'anointed one'. That is why, in the New Testament, when it is quoted, it says, 'The Lord and his Christ'. In the Old Testament your translation probably says, 'The Lord and his anointed'.

In the gospels you read in many places of many people chatting and asking, 'Do you think this is the Christ?' That was the word in common parlance. When Jesus asked the Pharisees whose son they thought Christ would be, they knew perfectly that Jesus was referring to all the prophecies which called him, 'the anointed one'. Everybody in Jesus' day used the Greek translation of the Old Testament and that translation had the name 'Christ' where the Hebrew had 'the anointed one'.

▼ CHECKPOINTS ▼

JESUS IN THE PSALMS

Ten Psalms Give Thirty details, 1,000 years before fulfilment 'David wrote of me—inspired by Holy Spirit' Matthew 22:43

Called 'Christ' means anointed. Matthew 26:63.
Psalm 2:2 'The Lord and his anointed' or 'his Christ' Psalm 45:7

Rejected by earth's rulers Psalm 2:2; rulers plot against Christ

Begotten from The Dead. When?
Psalm 2:7 'This day'—the Resurrection Day
Psalm 118:17—26 Rejected stone became head, on The Lord's day v.24.
Will return v.26
Colossians 1:18 'First-born from the dead'
Acts 13:33 'This God fulfilled by raising Jesus from the dead, as it is written [in Ps. 2], you are my son, This day have I begotten you'
1 Corinthians 15:23 First in order of resurrection; 'first-born from the dead'
Revelation 1:15 'First-born from the dead.'

Pre-existence
The Son existed before this from eternity: 'I am' John 8:58

Earthly Reign
Psalm 2:7–9 'The earth your possession...with a rod of iron'
'Rod of iron' to be experienced by opponents of Christ; Revelation 19:15
Matthew 25:31 'He will sit on his glorious throne'
Matthew 6:10 Lord's Prayer 'Your kingdom come...*on earth*'
Psalm 45:6 'Your throne is forever and ever'

His Gracious words prophesied in Psalm 45
Psalm 45:2 'Grace poured into your lips'
Luke 4:22 'Gracious words' John 7:46 'No one spoke like this man'
'Fairer' Hebrew word twice 'Beautiful, beautiful'; lovely character.
'A sceptre of righteousness, is the sceptre of his kingdom' v.6
Myrrh v.8 anoints for his death on the cross
Cassia anoints bread for lovely taste. Bread of life satisfies
Aloes gives fragrance to those near Christ

Marriage of the Bride Psalm 45:9–17
ie. Those won to Christ, Revelation 19:7–9

The Missing Words

Do you enjoy supplying missing words in a competition? I do! Lots of people spend hours supplying the missing letters in a crossword puzzle.

Did you know that the Bible has a missing words puzzle for you? It is in Psalm 40.

What do you do when working on a crossword? You look at the clues! Where should you look for the clues in the Bible? Well, in the New Testament, of course. In this case, you will find the clue where this verse is quoted in the New Testament. It is the letter to the Hebrews, chapter 10:5. 'Sacrifice and offering you did not desire'.

The next words should supply the missing ones in the

Old Testament. What are they—'A body you have prepared for me.'

How remarkable! Remarkable because that Psalm 40 was a prophecy made by David, 1,000 years before Jesus came to fulfil it!

But can we be sure that the words in the New Testament were not added after they were fulfilled? Do you know how we can know they were the genuine original words? It is because they were in the Greek translation of the Old Testament, and this Greek translation was made 288 years before Christ came, and that was the version all the people used in Christ's time. Yes, those words are there. 'A body you have prepared for me'. So what a great solution to the missing words. They could be a solution to words missing in someone's life! Could they be these? 'Lord Jesus, thank you that your body was prepared for suffering in my place. I accept forgiveness through your sacrifice'.

▼ CHECKPOINTS ▼

PROPHETIC PSALMS 22, 40, 110 AND 118

Psalm 40

Supply the missing words from Psalm 40:46:
Jewish Hebrew copy of AD900 had lost the words)
'Sacrifice you did not desire _____
burnt offering and sin offering you have not required.'

- Clue from New Testament Greek in Hebrews 10:5:
  Sacrifice you did not desire *soma de katertiso moi*
- Clue from Old Testament Greek LXX translated 280BC
  Sacrifice you did not desire *soma de Katertiso moi*
- Clue from the Dead Sea Scroll 100BC agrees. So they supply the words which are missing from the Hebrew copy of AD900.
  The English translation is: *But a body you prepared for me.*

Significance of Psalm 40
David 1000BC heard the second person of the Trinity prophecy that a body would be prepared for him (by virgin conception) for him to sacrifice for our sins.
'And in the volume of the book it is prophesied of me.'

What volume was that?
Up to David's time it was the Pentateuch, Joshua, Judges, to 1 Kings. Scrolls were by Moses, Joshua and Samuel, all put in the sanctuary (Deut. 31:24–26; Josh. 24—26; 1 Sam. 10:25). Moses wrote of atoning sacrifice and Samuel of Kingship.

Psalm 22
Describes suffering in detail of Christ on the cross. Mark each detail. Can you find twenty-four?

Psalm 118
Three things prophesied: the joyful Resurrection, The Lord's day, and foundation stone for faith.

Psalm 110
Ascension to God's right hand until his return, and our present advocate. It is a private conversation in heaven which David overheard. The Father and the Son were discussing future plans.

---

31 | The Future Foretold

What God Foretold to Hosea

Most commentaries miss the main point of Hosea's tragedy. It is that, even as Hosea places his wife on probation for a long time, so God would place Israel on probation for over two millenial days in their dispersion.

God's Broken Home

Did you know that God had a broken home and a broken heart? This will help you if you have experienced this close at hand. Today, most families have had an experience of this in some way—either one of their sons or daughters has experienced it, or a relative, or sadly their own marriage has been threatened.

Yes, I said that God had a broken home. That is what he told Hosea the prophet. 'O the pain of it!' said God, 'I had a wife who left me her husband, and she became a prostitute, not once, not twice, but three times. And now I have still taken her back but this time I have put her on probation.

'But Hosea, you must show compassion and forgiveness for your unfaithful wife; for I will show compassion for Israel, after she has learnt her lesson, after her period of probation. Her period of probation will be 2,500 years and I will bring back her sons. I will not be defeated! I will win them back in the end. Where once I said, "You are not my wife or my sons", there (back in Israel) I will say, "My wife" and she will say, "My husband".'

'He has torn us and he will heal us. He has smitten us and he will bandage us up'. God said, 'This hurt me more than it hurt you', and he says the same to individuals. He says the same to you. 'Afterward the children of Israel will return and seek the Lord their God.'

So you have seen that if you have had the agony of a broken home or children with broken homes, God shares the agony. He will heal your backslidings, he says, he loves you freely.

There will be a happy ending to your story, even as we see God today working out a happy ending for Israel.

▼ CHECKPOINTS ▼

WHAT GOD FORETOLD TO HOSEA

Significance missed by most commentaries:
That just as Hosea put his unfaithful wife on probation, so God was going to put, unfaithful Israel on probation for 2 millenial days (6:2) until purified by persecution then they would return to Palestine.

Hosea the first prophet
(775BC to apply warnings of Leviticus 26 (Seven Times) dispersion. Northern 10 tribes, called Ephraim or Israel, were worse than Judah

Brief prophesied history in chapter one
1. Ephraim will go into captivity before Judah (v.6)
2. Judah to be saved (v.7) from Assyria's invasion, by divine intervention not by arms (fulfilled 2 Kgs. 19:6–8)
3. God would bring them back, even as Hosea would win back his wife. They would return to The Land where God had disowned them (v.10)
4. Both Ephraim and Judah would return to the Holy Land under 'One Head' (v.11) in the latter days (Ezek. 37:15–23)

Probation period chapter 3 onwards
To be purified by Persecution
Remarkable fulfilment predicted in 3:4—5
• Israel has existed without king or country
• without idolatry
• without sacrifices (they ended in AD70)
• without priests (ended AD70)
They are returning to Palestine in the Latter Days
Their loving God will welcome back the prodigal Israel.
'I will heal their backslidings. I will love them freely' (14:4)

Replacements during probation prepared for the Gospel
Synagogues replaced Temple
Rabis replaced Priests
Christ's Atonement replaced animal sacrifices

Ezekiel's Fatal Haircut
Tied up in Ezekiel's hair was the world's history and
Israel's destiny. Let your hair down by reading the clues
which God gives to those of a teachable spirit.

The hair-raising illustration is in chapter 5. God gave
an outline of history which was still future for Ezekiel.
The rest of the prophecy was worked out in chronological order throughout the rest of the book, and inter-
twined with it is the departure and return of God's glory
to the Holy Land.

The first chapter opens with the vision of God's glory
hovering over Jerusalem. Reluctantly his glory moves
out stage by stage. Each stage gives Judah an opportunity to respond to God's pleading, but it always falls on
deaf ears. Finally the glory departs from the Mount of
Olives. It only returns there at the end of the age in
chapter 43.

At what point have today's events reached in this
order? We are at the end of chapter 37 with Israel back
in the Holy Land with the two tribes and ten tribes

united as one nation. The next events to be fulfilled are described in chapters 38 to 48.

It may be asked, 'Were these chapters of Ezekiel written so long ago, meant to refer to our times?' The answer is 'yes'. It is admitted that the invasion described in chapters 38 and 39 have never yet happened. This confirms the scripture which says it will be fulfilled 'after many days...in the latter years,' and it will be when Israel has returned and settled down in 'God's Land' after a long period of desolation (vv.8 and 12).

The nations in chapter 38:2-6 have been identified in *Young's Concordance*, *Hasting's Dictionary* and by Professor H. Hawkes of Oxford who is an authority on East European ethnology. Those north of the Black Sea were of the Halstatt horse culture. Others were Iran, Iraq, Libya, Ethiopia, Samaliland, and Germany.

▼ CHECKPOINTS ▼

WHAT GOD FORETOLD TO EZEKIEL

A Hair-raising prophecy

Chapter 5, a comprehensive prophecy from Ezekiel for 26 centuries. The prophet's hair divided into three portions, represents Israel's future.

1. Two portions represent those burnt or slain in the invasion of 603 to 586 (v.2)
2. One third of Judah will survive but is scattered to the winds (v.12), 22:153.
3. A little hair is rescued from that scattered, symbolising a remnant who would return to Jerusalem after 70 years exile (533BC (v.3)
4. Even these the prophet then throws into the fire. The Romans will scatter them because they reject Christ (v.4) Fulfilled by fall of Jerusalem AD70
5. All the scattered third will return to Israel at the end of the age. It began in 1917

Note: Principle that a prophetic day equals one year is in chapter 4

Fits into Theme of God's Glory, which structures the whole prophecy.

Opening vision of glory chapter 1. Stage by stage glory reluctantly departs as Judah refuses to repent of her cruel horrible practises and idolatry.

- 1st The Glory lifts up from the ark chapter 9
- 2nd From the sanctuary entrance to the east gate (10:18)
- 3rd From the Mount of Olives the glory departs (11:23)

Meanwhile

Israel will have little sanctuaries (Synagogues) through the world (11:16).

Israel is left as a valley of dry bones (37:1)

Israel is revived and return as united 12 tribes to Holy Land (37:15–23)

When settled they will be invaded (Armageddon?)

Israel will recognise the Lord and pagan nations are judged (39:21)

'They will see my glory' at the return of Christ

- 4th **The Glory returns** via Olivet on the East (43:1) Cf. Zech. 14:4; Acts 1:11,12
- 5th Through the East gate 'The earth shone with his glory'
- 6th Into the house of The Lord 'Lo! The Glory of The Lord filled the house.' 'Son of man, this is the place of my throne.' (43:5,6) (Matt. 25:31,32)

What God Told Daniel: The Gentile Future

The formation of a States of Europe soon before Christ's return is also a sign given. It has been so clear in Holy Scripture that believers have written about it for the last hundred years, eg. the fourth empire of Daniel's image in chapter 2 is the iron Roman empire.

This is divided into two as depicted by the two legs, the western and the eastern Empire; then the ten toes depict an amalgamation of those countries in the last days.

It is soon before the return of Christ, because God said, 'In the days of those kings, he will set up a kingdom which will never be destoyed'. How? It will be by the stone uncreated which will descend from heaven and smash the image on its toes. The toes represent the last European power to exist before Christ's descent from heaven.

This amalgam, of European powers will be that of separate sovereign states, because it says, 'In the days of those kings'. Note the plural. That is why when the picture is repeated in Revelation 13, the one crown is taken from the one emperor and placed as separate crowns upon each of the ten heads of the beast. It is interesting that even European nations which have no king as such, still refer to themselves as sovereign states.

First Coming or Second Coming?

How do we know that this stone which smashed the image on its feet means the second coming and not the first coming? It is because at his second coming, he will descend visibly from heaven. That is what the stone did. He did not do that at his first coming. He came then as a baby—as God incarnate.

Another sign that this refers to the second coming is that it is to happen later in history, after the height of

Rome's power. The Roman Empire, Daniel said, will have become divided and then split into many European countries and finally an amalgamation of several countries into a States of Europe. It is 'In the days of those powers', that the uncreated stone descends from heaven and smashes the image of man's governmental systems and sets up a kingdom of godliness, righteousness and happiness.

The Times of the Gentiles

Did you know that Jesus called the Emperor's dream statue in the book of Daniel, The Times of the Gentiles. It is that 25 centuries since Babylonian Empire down to our day which the Lord Jesus Christ calls the time of the Gentiles. He calls it that in Luke 21:24.

Why is it called, 'The Times of the Gentiles?' It is because during that time, Gentiles have ruled in Jerusalem. Its duration is the same period as the dispersion of Israel. For the same 25 centuries, the Israelites have been scattered among countries other than their own, as prophesied.

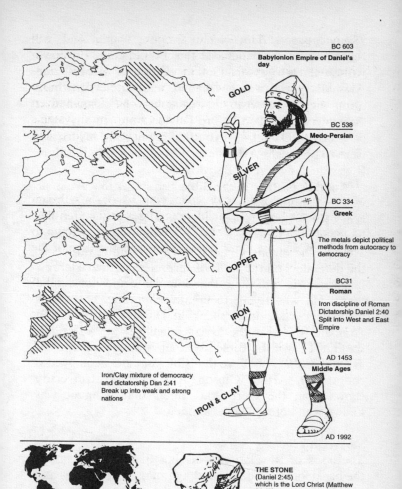

BC 603
Babylonian Empire of Daniel's day

GOLD

BC 538
Medo-Persian

SILVER

BC 334
Greek

The metals depict political methods from autocracy to democracy

COPPER

BC 31
Roman

Iron discipline of Roman Dictatorship Daniel 2:40 Split into West and East Empire

IRON

AD 1453
Middle Ages

Iron/Clay mixture of democracy and dictatorship Dan 2:41 Break up into weak and strong nations

IRON & CLAY

AD 1992

THE STONE
(Daniel 2:45)
which is the Lord Christ (Matthew 21:42)

Fig 21 Daniel's image prophesying history from 630BC to the present day

The Language of Babylon

At one time, the critics said that Daniel could not have written those chapters (2:4 to chapter 8) because the Aramaic speech was not known until later. But there again they were wrong. Archaeology has shown that Aramaic was spoken before David's time. In any case, chapter 1 of Daniel tells you that Daniel and his friends were to be taught Aramaic as part of their re-education. It was the language of Babylon.

Another passage in the Bible also shows that Aramaic was spoken long before Daniel—200 years in fact. This is in 2 Kings 18:26. It was when Good King Hezekiah was beseiged in Jerusalem by the triumphant Assyrian armies. The enemy General started shouting threats to the defenders on the walls of Jerusalem in their Hebrew language. He told them that Jehovah could not defend them. He was trying to create a mutiny. The king's messenger said, don't speak in Hebrew but speak in Aramaic (that was the Syrian language) for we understand it. Now if the Bible says that Aramaic was spoken as early as that, I believe the Bible, but archaeology also confirms it. Arthur Gibson of Manchester University shows from the Dere Ala tablets that Aramaic was known well before Daniel's time.

Sovereign Teaching

The book of Revelation proclaims this teaching amidst the backcloth of thunder and lightning, roaring seas and scorching sun, earthquakes and the sound of trumpets. The rise and fall of kings and empires is summed up by this comment in Revelation 17:17.

> 'God has put it into their hearts to fulfil his purpose, to be of one mind in giving their kingdom to the beast, until the words of God are fulfilled'.

Consequently, whether the Emperor was good or bad, Peter said in 1 Peter 2:13,14 'Submit yourselves to every ordinance of man for the Lord's sake, whether to the king as supreme, or to governors... for this is the will of God, that by doing good you may silence the ignorant misrepresentations of foolish men'.

Paul likewise said in Romans 13:1–2, 'Be subject unto the authorities... for they are ordained by God'.

Concerning the prophesied future, he wrote, 'He who now restrains, will do so until he is removed, and then the lawless one will be revealed whom the Lord will consume away with the breath of his mouth (his inspired word) and finally destroy with the brightness of his coming'.

▼ CHECKPOINTS ▼

WHAT GOD FORETOLD TO DANIEL

The Gentile future and prophesied history of the Four Empires form 603BC to 20th century

Note: the Aramaic language was in use well before Daniel's time

Images of the Empires (Dan.2)	Animal Symbols of Empires (Dan.7)
Head of Gold = Babylon 603—538BC	Deflated Lion = Nebuchadnezzar humbled by madness
Arms and Chest of Silver = Medo Persia 538–334BC	Lop-sided Bear = Persia stronger than Media. 3 ribs: Egypt, Babylon, Lydia defeated
Waist of Bronze = Greece 334–31BC	Leopard with 4 wings = Alexander who dies and 4 Generals divide Empire

Legs of Iron = Rome 31BC to 20 Century AD. Divides into E and W like the legs then into ten (toes) at the end (European single market with 10 ethnic groupings?	The Horror Beast with iron teeth. Europe breaks up into 10 'kingdoms'. Little horn propaganda uproots 3 kingdoms. After 3½ times (1,260 years) Bible read again and gradually corrects errors 7:25,26
Uncreated stone descends from Heaven in days of ten toes and smashes The Image	Son of Man descends with the clouds

God's Sovereignty is the prime teaching in Daniel. Man proposes but God disposes, or 'human randomness mutates into Divine teleology (purpose).'

Each episode reaches this conclusion:
- Daniel's image 2:21 'God removes Kings and sets up Kings'
- Monarch's Madness 4:32 'The most high overrules in the kingdoms of men'
- Writing on the wall 5:21 'The most high overrules in the kingdoms of men'
- Lion's Den 6:26,27 'God's Kingdom cannot be destroyed'
- Horror Beast 7:21–27 Wears out saints only until 'Judgement sits'
- Waiting for Messiah 9:24 'Seventy weeks of years are *determined*'

NT applies this sovereign teaching
Revelation 17 'God has put it into their hearts to fulfill his will…until'
1 Peter 2:13,14 'Submit yourselves…unto governors as sent by him'
Romans 13: 1,2 'Be subject unto the authorities…they are ordained by God'

What God Foretold To Daniel: in Hebrew Confidentiality

When will the Sanctuary be Cleansed?
Chapters 8 to 12 are an answer to the question, 'When will the Sanctuary be cleansed?' In answering this, it involves the Jewish future and is therefore confidential. This is why Daniel was inspired to write these chapters in the old Hebrew which was no longer in general use, but understood by Jews.

The future fortunes of the Jews and the Sanctuary

where the Temple stood were in an area which was going to be invaded by the Greek king, Alexander the Great, 200 years after God told Daniel about it. That is why the scene is set in the area which was going to be covered by the Greek Empire. This Empire was symbolised by the goat which is appropriate because the sea between Greece and Turkey is called the Goat Sea or Aegean in the Greek. After AD638, the area of the Greek Empire was occupied by Moslem powers who extended their conquests to Yugoslavia and the Balkans in AD1453. So these prophesies extend down to our time.

Historic Purposes

In the prophecies God gave to Daniel, we have seen the purpose behind each Empire down the last 2,500 years. You see, God didn't foretell the future just to satisfy curiosity. It was to show his purpose behind history.

The Persian Empire restored a remnant of godly people back to Palestine after 70 years as foretold by Jeremiah. The temple was rebuilt and so were the city walls. That remnant established Jewry which prepared for Christ's first coming.

The Greek Empire which followed—what was God's purpose for them? What language was your New Testament written in? It was Greek. All translations of the New Testament are translations from the Greek, which had become the international language of the day.

Alexander the Great spread his conquests East and West. Even in Egypt the language became Greek. That is why even the Old Testament became translated into Greek 280 years before Christ. By the time of Christ, the Greek version of the Old Testament was widely used even by the Jews. It was from this translation that all the Christians quoted when they wrote the New Testament.

The surprising thing is that even when the Greek

Empire gave way to the Roman Empire, the international language still continued to be Greek. That is why Paul and others had this international language to use when they travelled through Europe.

So what about the Roman Empire? How did God use that iron empire? Rome's iron might removed all national barriers. Passports were not needed to pass from country to country. Rome's roads, too, took the traveller from one end of Europe to another. Paul was able to travel freely to bring the good news of salvation and so did the other Christians.

Remember that the prophecies of Daniel said that the Roman Empire would later divide up into about ten countries. This it did, so what purpose did God have in that? Was it not so that these European countries could send explorers throughout the world? Unintentionally that opened up the world for Christians to take the good news. When the countries fail to help the gospel, God withdraws his blessing. If we look at history through Bible eyes, we shall understand.

▼ CHECKPOINTS ▼

CONFIDENTIAL HEBREW LANGUAGE ABOUT JEW'S FUTURE

Temple Sanctuary Cleansing chapters 8 to 12 of Daniel
God's Computer Angel named Palmoni 'wonderful calculator'
Sanctuary was in the former Greek Empire (Dan. 8:21,22)

Palmoni says 2,300 years before cleansing begins.
333BC to 1967 = 2,300 years. Wailing Wall made a synagogue.
Sanctuary Cycle is an amazing cycle (M. de Cheseaux's astronomical discovery)

Three Abominations:
1. Antiochus Epiphanes 167BC sacrilege in temple (8:23)
2. Fall of Jerusalem. Roman and Zealot sacrilege of temple. Jesus and Daniel spoke of another after no.1 (Matt. 24:15)

3. Mosque 'Standing where it ought not' AD638 (11:31). But some refer it to the tribulation.

Messiah dated 70 weeks of days, ie. 490 years (Dan. 9:25,26) **fulfilled:**

457BC Cyrus commands to build temple (9:25 and Ezra 1:2)
+ 490 **solar** years = AD33 the Cross
444BC Artaxerxes commands building of the walls + 490 **lunar** years = AD33 (Neh. 2:1,5).

Christ was crucified in the middle of last week of years, ie. after 3½ year ministry; that reduces AD33 to AD30.

Signs of Christ's second coming in chapter 12
1. When Resurrection of believers is near (12:2)
2. Terrible time of trouble (12:1)
3. Increased travel, invention and science for many (12:4)
4. It will be the end of 7 times (3½ × 2) (ch. 12:7) in 20th century
5. Great increase in wickedness (12:10) but bright witnessing
6. From Moslem date to blessing Israel 1335 = 1917 Home for Jews (12:11,12)
7. The Wise will understand these figures in the last days (12:9,10)

What God Foretold To Zechariah

Introduction to Zechariah–An Astonishing Statement

I want to draw out your imagination of the events which led up to the next to last book of the Old Testament. It is the book of the prophet Zechariah. It is a dramatic book, written from 520 to 517BC. **It actually pictures Jehovah being crucified on the Cross.** The Hebrew says, 'it is me, Jehovah, whom they pierced', and the whole Israelite nation will be converted when they see it is me whom they crucified when I return to the Mount of Olives at the end of the age (Zech. 12:10 and 14:3,4).

Earth-shaking Events

I have already described God's geological knowledge in Volume 2. The earth-shaking events which are to happen at Christ's return are described to Ezekiel in such a way as to show that God knew all about the geology of this globe. It will involve the great rift valley and the movement of continents. It reveals that the increase in earthquakes is the continents preparing to split at the moment Christ's feet touch the Mount of Olives at his descent. The dramatic results are described in chapter 47 and in Zechariah 14.

Zechariah 14:4 says it will be, I quote, 'On that day his feet will stand on the Mount of Olives which lies before Jerusalem on the East'.

Whose feet are these? Verse 3 tells you they are Jehovah's (which is translated 'The Lord'). In the New Testament you are told that they will be the feet of the Lord Jesus Christ. Clearly this implies that Jesus is Jehovah.

Now turn to Acts 1:11 and you read that two angels appeared to the disciples as the Lord Jesus ascended into heaven. They said, 'Men of Galilee, why do you stand looking into heaven? This same Jesus, who is taken up from you into heaven, will come in the same manner that you have seen him go into heaven'.

It is then that two great geological events will happen of cataclysmic proportions.

1. A great rift valley will open up past Jerusalem and link up the Mediterranean Sea with the Red Sea and the Indian Ocean.

2. Fresh water will be released from an artesian basin which is known to be under Jerusalem.

Now note that these events are associated with the Lord becoming king over all the earth (v.9) Why? Because it will make Jerusalem the maritime centre of the world. In fact Zechariah, like the other prophets, ends with Christ reigning in a millenium of peace for all creation.

▼ CHECKPOINTS ▼

WHAT GOD FORETOLD TO ZECHARIAH

List of Prophecies about Jesus' first coming:

Palm Sunday: Jesus will ride on donkey to temple now being built (9:9)

Betrayed for 30 pieces of silver (11:12,13)

Jesus as God The Good Shepherd (13:7)

He will be Jehovah whom they crucify (12:10)

He will be the chief stone of salvation bringing Grace (4:7)

He is the Branch of David's fallen tree (3:8; 6:12)

He is Priest-King descended through Zerubbabel (6:13; 4:6–10; Matt. 1:12)

Events of the last days described in last four chapters:

1. Revival in the latter rain (10:1)
2. Return of Israel from all the world (10:10)
3. Lebanon's agony (11:1,2)
4. Problems of Jerusalem brings failure to politicians (12:3)
5. Army from all nations will attack Jerusalem (12:3)
6. Christ will suddenly descend to Mount Olivet (12:10; 14:4)
7. Israelis will recognise Christ's wounds (TV close-up?) (12:12)
8. Israel's sorrow, repentance and cleansing (12:10–14)
9. Christ will descend when city is half taken (14:1–4)
10. Olivet will split in two and rift valley joins up Mediterranean (14:4–8)
11. Christ will judge the world and reign over it (14:9)
12. Every nation will send up representatives to worship Jesus Christ at Harvest Festival time (14:16–19)
13. All adverts, newspapers and TV will be cleansed and only propogate pure and wholesome things (14:20,21)

32 | The Prince of Prophets

You will of course immediately recognise that the Prince of Prophets is the Lord Jesus. His major prophecy given on the Mount of Olives is the most remarkable outline of history ever predicted which was to happen between his ascension and his return.

Many events he prophesied are now facts of history and others are unfolding before us, but some people get confused because they say there are all kinds of opinion about application. Others just weigh one opinion against another. This is not the way to get the truth from God's Word. Behind differing opinions, we should look for the motives and assumptions behind such opinions. For example, some *don't* believe that the Lord Jesus will personally appear in the heavens. Others are more wedded to the passing fashions of theological thought.

So, to be subject to the insight of the Holy Spirit and carefully comparing scripture with scripture, we have to let self be crucified. St. Paul says in 2 Corinthians 10:5, 'Cast down all theories and every pride that exalts itself...and bring into captivity every thought to obey Christ'.

So you see, it is not just a matter of weighing up man's opinions but noting carefully the *terms of reference* in the scriptures themselves and subjecting even our own pet theories to Christ.

What are the terms of reference in what Jesus, the Prince of Prophets, said about the future? Turn with me to Matthew 24. This remarkable prophecy by the Lord himself is also reported in Mark 13 and Luke 21 but we will look now at Matthew 24:3. Here we find that the Lord Jesus answers three questions put to him by the disciples.

1. When will Jerusalem and the temple be destroyed?
2. What will be the signs of your second coming?
3. What will be the signs of the end of the age?

As a matter of fact, if we see that the Saviour was replying to those three questions, what he said outlines the history of the 2,000 years from his time to ours.

▼ CHECKPOINTS ▼

THE LORD JESUS CHRIST

Jesus answered 3 questions: 1. Jerusalem; 2. The Age; 3. Second coming
Jesus Foretells 20 centuries of history in Matthew 24 and 25; Mark 13; Luke 21

1. **When would Jerusalem Fall?** (It was in AD70)
First the disciples would have to witness.
Then there would be two stages in fall:
AD67 When 'Wars of Jews' began. Cestius surrounds the city.
Christians must flee whole country because 3½ years war would commence; this is recorded by Luke alone
AD70 Titus would reach Jerusalem at Passover. Christians must flee over roof tops, last minute (Matt. and Mk.). Jews tribulation follows and Jerusalem trodden down until AD67 (Lk. 24:24)

2. **The Age** would not end until 'Times of the Gentiles' ended (Lk. 24:24). Two main apostacies would last 1,260 years and 1,335: one in West 'inner rooms'. One in East 'Prophet of Desert' Matthew 24:26

The Jewish Tribulation would last from the fall of Jerusalem until the second coming (Lk. 21:22–24, Matt. 24:21,29)

3. Signs of second coming

Space signs (Matt. 24:29; Mk. 13:24; Lk. 21:25)
Increase in earthquakes, famine and epidemics
World wars involving whole populations
Organisation of nations to solve problems (Lk. 21:25)
Uranium nuclear fission (heavens—Greek *uranos*) (Mk. 13:25)
Phobias and stress at threat
Fig tree (Israel) reviving and returning to 'God's Land'
Sign of Son of Man coming in the clouds
Matthew 25
a. Wedding of Bride—ie. The saved (resurrection) (Matt. 24:40–42)
b. Rewards and places in coming Kingdom
c. Christ's throne on earth to judge nations Kingdom on earth follows (Lk. 21:31).

33 | The Risen Jesus Foretells the Future

The Triumphal Arch of Revelation

At the entrance to Thessalonica in Northern Greece, there is an ancient Arch of Triumph. It shows a series of pictures of the Emperor Galerius in AD310. It was actually his last triumph because he was a cruel persecutor of Christians. Ironically, his huge tomb nearby became a meeting place for Christians and for a thousand years they met to praise and worship the triumphant Christ.

The last book in the Bible is like an arch of triumph — the triumph and victory of tthe Lord Jesus Christ. Likewise, there is a panel of pictures. Each panel ends in a victory for Jesus. That is why the book is called 'The Revelation' — the Revelation of Jesus Christ. That is what the opening words call this remarkable book: 'The Revelation of Jesus Christ which God gave unto him to show to his servants'.

As I studied the panels on that earthly triumphal arch, I saw there were some symbols which I didn't understand; but other pictures were quite clear in their meaning. For example, some soldiers were mounted on horses just as it is in the Revelation panel and at the end of each panel the emperor was in his victory chariot. It is the same in the book of Revelation. The Lord Jesus is on his triumphant throne or in his victory procession at the end of each panel. Then comes the final conquest and his eternal reign.

▼ CHECKPOINTS ▼

TRIUMPHAL ARCH OF REVELATION

Prophesies world history from 1st Century to modern times.

Analysis: Christ's triumphal arch has:

Four panels. Each panel has seven pictures and ends with Christ's triumph

Between each panel there are given symbols to explain meanings of the panels. eg. Revelation 17:1

1st Panel of seven lampstands ie. Christian witness. Matthew 5:15; Zechariah 4; Revelation 1:20

1st to 20th century

Christ witnessing amidst seven church eras

Vision of heaven's control room chapters 4 and 5

2nd Panel seven Seals Christ's triumph over Rome, chapters 6 and 7 AD62—323

Symbol of the martyrs, Hebrew and Gentile 7:1–17

Short space of peace before apostacies persecute 18:1

3rd Panel seven Trumpets persecution by the two Apostacies, chapters 8 to ten

Euphratean power floods out from East, chapter 9:14 sixth trumpet

Causes the Reformation in the West, chapter 10

Four symbols to interpret the panel, chapters 11 to 14

4th Panel seven Cauldrons of wrath defeat the apostacies

Each cauldron is a reply to each Trumpet in panel three

Euphratean power dries up. Chapter 16:12 sixth cauldron

Visions to explain the cauldrons 'One of the angels of the cauldrons came and said, "Come, I will show you..." ' (17:1)

Note The above is the **Historic** application of panels 1 to 4. The **Futuristic** fulfilment would be during The Tribulation. Prophecy is usually fulfilled both ways. ie. Symbolically and then literally (Matt. 17:10–13).

Seven Sisters

As I look along the beautiful cliffs towards Eastbourne in England, I see the chalk cliffs which are called the Seven Sisters. The cliffs shine white in the sun and the glistening sea laps at their bases. The sea eats away this base so that the chalk rock falls straight down. This leaves the white chalk cliffs always vertical and at the top the fresh grass grows a green carpet right to the edge. This gives the top a wavy green line emphasising the seven white humps. These are the Seven Sisters divided by six dips. The last dip before the seventh hump is wider than the others. Indeed, it is called a gap—Birling Gap. When I get to it, I look through it and . . . the cliffs turn a corner. They start a new series of white cliffs.

Now, in the book of Revelation, the seven seals and the trumpets are like that. In both cases, there is a gap between the sixth and the seventh. Into that gap is put a symbol or vision. This is to give an insight into the next series of sevens to follow. It is as if to say:

'You expected the end to come didn't you, but no, there is another seven to come, before the end'.

This is to keep the church expectant all down the ages. The church which no longer expects her Lord to return is a church which has fallen asleep. So said the Lord in his parable of the ten virgins.

What is that common feature in the seven trumpets? It is a time measurement. The prophecies of the seven trumpets concern a period of 1,260 days. Remember that Ezekiel was told that each day represented one year. So the seven trumpets concern a period of 1,260 years long.

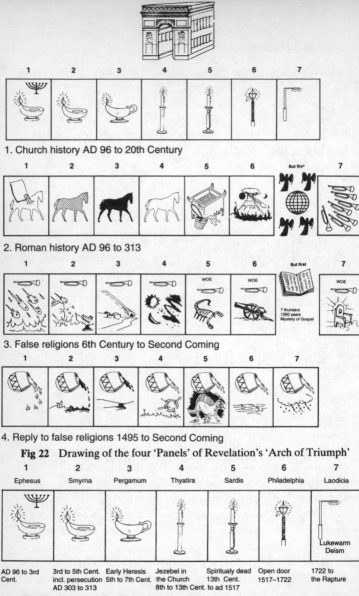

1. Church history AD 96 to 20th Century

2. Roman history AD 96 to 313

But first

7 thunders
1260 years
Mystery of Gospel

3. False religions 6th Century to Second Coming

4. Reply to false religions 1495 to Second Coming

Fig 22 Drawing of the four 'Panels' of Revelation's 'Arch of Triumph'

1	2	3	4	5	6	7
Ephesus	Smyrna	Pergamum	Thyatira	Sardis	Philadelphia	Laodicia

Lukewarm Deism

| AD 96 to 3rd Cent. | 3rd to 5th Cent. incl. persecution AD 303 to 313 | Early Heresis 5th to 7th Cent. | Jezebel in the Church 8th to 13th Cent. to ad 1517 | Spiritualy dead 13th Cent. to ad 1517 | Open door 1517–1722 | 1722 to the Rapture |

Fig 23 Panel of the Seven Lamp-stands

Fig 24 The symbols following the panel of the seven seals

The kingdom has not been won yet. That won't happen until the rapture of the saved—that is, until the resurrection of those born again. Wait until we have sealed the complete number.

Now, Ephesians 1:13 tells you what this sealing is. The believer is sealed by the Holy Spirit when he believes the gospel and is saved. Then chapter 4:30 tells you that that sealing guarantees that the bodies of the saved will be changed and resurrected at the coming of Christ.

So what is the angel saying in Revelation 7? There are many more centuries of history still to come after AD313 in which millions more will be saved and suffer death for Christ. Not till then will the saved be reaped. That is why we don't hear of the 144,000 again until seven chapters on, in chapter 14. Not until chapter 14 does the Lord Jesus put in his sickle and reap his wheat. In parables, the wheat always depicts the saved and the Lord is depicted as coming on a cloud with the souls of the saved in heaven to resurrect the living believers still on earth, as 1 Thessalonians 4 says.

What is the trademark of those believers? Revelation 14 tells you. They sing the new song! No unsaved person can sing that! They are those who have been redeemed.

Protection and Deliverance

What a comforting picture for days like these. Today politicians openly talk of the possible destruction of all life on earth. Revelation 7 opens with a picture of our planet being threatened with destruction. This destruction is on land and sea and a third of trees are destroyed. But four angels hold back this threat until the number to be saved is completed. Out world is certainly threatened but it should comfort you to know that God reigns.

In the book of Revelation, there is a pattern—a structure. The whole wonderful book is unfolded upon this structure. For example, after each panel of sevens, God gives illustrations or parables to show what the panels mean. Each panel ends in triumph for Jesus Christ.

Now, a word about parables. You should always remember that parables are only given as illustrations. How are we to know the truth from error? Most errors are founded upon favourite interpretations of obscure symbols. They are not given to teach doctrine. For doctrine we read the clear statements of the epistles and gospels.

34 | Triumphal Arch (1)

Warning Trumpets

I was watching a pagentry of ancient warfare. The watchman on the city tower suddenly blew his trumpet. It was to warn the whole fortress that the enemy was coming. The defenders were surprised. They thought they had already defeated the enemy in an earlier battle. The enemy advanced to attack the walls. The defenders tipped great iron bowls of scalding liquid upon the attackers. One by one the bowls were poured out and the enemy retreated. This is the picture in the next three chapters of Revelation from 7 to 9. Seven angels prepare to sound the warning that the battle is not over.

We have seen how that the seals of Revelation chapter 6 shows a great victory. They depicted how the Roman Empire was won to accept Christianity by the fourth century. Christians rejoiced that the great battle of martydom was over. The battle seemed to be won. The whole population of the Empire was actually encouraged to go to church.

But heaven saw it differently. The seven angel trumpeters were to sound the warnings one by one. Satan was not going to be defeated as easily as that. The heathen now flooded into the church. As the centuries went by, their pagan ideas contaminated the truth. Christ offered the water of life; those waters were not poisoned. Chapter 8:10 says a third of these waters were made bitter and many died.

Meanwhile, a fresh peril approaches as the next angel

sounds his trumpet. This fifth trumpet was a peril which was to wipe out all the churches of North Africa (Revelation 9).

You have probably guessed by now that the trumpets are warnings against false religion. Now look at our own churches. Even in churches where the gospel is clearly preached, there are many who have never personally received Christ into their hearts as Saviour. It is as necessary to evangelise your own congregations as it is to evangelise the world.

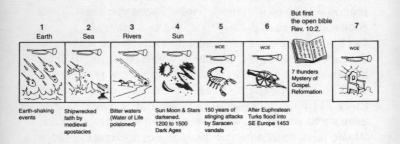

Fig 25 Panel of the Seven Trumpets

The Trumpets

We have seen how the fourth trumpet warned Christians of the Dark Ages, as they are called. Next, the fifth trumpet warned the church of the prophet of the desert—the false prophet which deceived many. It warned Christians of the Saracen invasion which was to sweep through Northern Africa and kill Christians and demolish the church.

The description of the devastating locusts of the fifth trumpet Dr Basil Atkinson identifies as the Saracen armies which swept like locusts out of Arabia about the year AD613 and over-ran Syria, Egypt, Persia, North Africa and even into Spain.

This sixth trumpet was even a worse blow at Christendom, worse that the Saracen woe (Rev. 9:12). The Euphratean power (The Turkish Empire) was unleased in 1055 (v. 12 onwards). This woe is symbolised by the River Euphrates. But the attack on European Christianity was to be held back for nearly 400 years until the attack on Constantinople in 1453 (according to 9:15); Ezekiel said that each day in prophecy represents a year in history and the total of one year and one month and one day and one hour is therefore 396 years—or nearly 400 years.

This capital of Eastern Christianity fell because the Turks introduced gunpowder and cannon-fire. This is described in 9:17,18. At Istanbul today, you can see these ancient cannons displayed at the railway station. The gun muzzels were shaped like lions and the smoke of gunfire would belch out of their mouths when the cannon was fired, just as described in Revelation 9.

Verse 17 describes gunpowder very accurately fourteen centuries before it was invented. From out of the mouths of cannons 'issued fire, smoke and sulphur'. *The Oxford Dictionary* says, 'Gunpowder, an explosive of saltpetre, charcoal and sulphur'. The word in the Greek for smoke is *kaptos*, which the Greek lexicon defines as from the verb *kaptoo*, to burn to charcoal which gives off smoke. So 'fire, charcoal smoke, and sulphur' is a very close identification of the new military machine which fired at the walls of Constantinople (Istanbul), demolished them after 396 years attempt, and broke through into south-east Europe.

The Ottoman military language is also described in these verses. They numbered their regiments by the term 'myriads' and this is the very word in the Greek of Revelation 9:16. This Turkish military word is used nowhere else in scripture. Notice the description of these horsemen. They had breastplates of fiery zeal, hyacinth blue, and sulphur yellow. This was the well-known armour colour of the Turkish soldiers.

Bible Rediscovered

But Satan overstepped himself. The fall of Constantinople was a rebuke to the church's idolatry, as God said, but it also caused the Greek Orthodox monks to flee to the West and bring with them the neglected Bible to be read and translated.

When the scholars of the western church began to translate them, they found a treasure beyond their wildest dreams. They could rejoice in a complete salvation accomplished by Christ on the cross. No longer did they have to whip themselves with metalled thongs, no longer did they have to wear prickly hair shirts in order to merit salvation. Christ had already saved them. He gave them abundant life as a free gift.

This next phase in Revelation 10:1 is represented by a mighty angel coming down from heaven with a rainbow around him, his face bright as the sun and a little book open in his hand. The Reformation indeed became the

time of the open book. People were allowed to read it
again.

▼ CHECKPOINTS ▼

SEVEN TRUMPETS AND SEVEN BOWLS

5th Trumpet Revelation 9:1–12

Saracens almost wipe out the great North African church;
vv.7–9 describe their famed horses, yellow turbans like
crowns of gold, manlike beards, but womanlike long hair.
Spiritual name v. 11 in Hebrew because they overran Palestine, and Greek because it was Greek Orthodox Church
which suffered.
Duration 150 years (5 mths v.5) AD613–763 then settled.
Then another 150 years (v.10) AD846–1096 of fresh
attacks on North Mediterranean.

6th Trumpet Revelation 9:13–21 Second great woe, a worse
blow to Christianity.

Turks launched their conquests from Bagdad in AD1057
Restrained from SE Europe for 396 years (v.15) until 1453
Cannon and gunpowder (new weapon v.17) breached
walls of Constantinople. (Gunpowder is made from chemi-
cals of v.17—saltpetre, charcoal and sulphur)
SE Europe subjugated. Monks flee to West with old scrip-
tures.
Reformation chapter 10 Translations from old scriptures
bring an open Bible recommission.
'A little book open' 'Take it...preach again to the nations'

Cauldrons (Bowls of Wrath) reverse the Trumpet apostacies

Reply to 1st Apostacy of Trumpets 1—4 and 2nd Apostacy
5,6.

▶ TRIUMPHAL ARCH (1)   181

Angel of the cauldrons shows John the meaning of everything from

Chapters 15 to 22; Cf. Revelation 17:1; 21:9; 22:1

The False bride in red claiming to be the Church chapters 17 to 19:4

The true bride in white 19:5–9

The Return of her groom, the King of Kings 19:11–18

The two apostacies finally demolished v.19–21

Satan chained during millenium 20:1–3

Christ's reign for 1,000 years

Final Judgement Day 20:11–15; John 5:29

The Bride's heaven 21:9 to 22:17

The Bride's invitation to the wedding 22:17

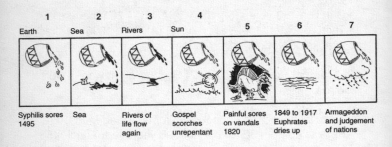

1	2	3	4	5	6	7
Earth	Sea	Rivers	Sun			
Syphilis sores 1495	Sea	Rivers of life flow again	Gospel scorches unrepentant	Painful sores on vandals 1820	1849 to 1917 Euphrates dries up	Armageddon and judgement of nations

Fig 26 Panel of the Seven Bowls

THE NEXT CENTURY

The Rapture

- Illustrated in Revelation is the first Resurrection. Those who believed
  The Wheat harvest in Spring—Christ's Wheat are those who die in the Lord (Rev. 14:13–16)
  The Grapes and fruit harvest in autumn is the second resurrection, ie. The ungodly for judgement (14:17–20; 20:5, 11–15 [cf. 1 Cor. 15:25–26]).
  One of the plagues was destructive Bible criticism (15:3). Victory was gained over them by those who sang the song of Moses and The Lamb, ie. Moses' writings were genuine and The Lamb's atonement fully effective (says Dr Basil Atkinson).
- Rapture next illustrated in chapter 16:15 before Armageddon in v.16 (cf. Isa. 26:19–21)
  'I am coming like a thief' This simile is used 5 times:
  1. Revelation 16:15
  2. Matthew 24:43 'Shall gather his elect'
  3. 1 Thessalonians 5:2 Children of light should not be surprised (v.4,5)
  4. 2 Peter 3:10 'Be blameless' (v.14)
  5. Revelation 3:3 Unworthy Christians warned as in 1 Corinthians 3:8–15
- Rapture next mentioned in 20:6 'This is the first Resurrection' (cf. 1 Peter 4:17)

The Millenium Revelation 20:2–7

- When? Opinion not essential. Love is more important (1 Cor. 13:2)
- Pointers:
  1. Kingdom comes after Christ's return (Lk. 31:31; Zech. 14:9–12; Joel 3:12–18; Hab. 2:14; Dan. 7:13–14)

2. Peace in creation follows Christians resurrection (Rom. 8:19-23)
3. Described in other scriptures 1 and 2 Peter 'age-lasting day' of 1,000 years
   Isaiah 2:2-4; Micah 4:1-8. Wars cease
   Isaiah 11:6-9; 65:17-25. Peace among animals
4. Before Christ's return, things get worse not better (2 Tim. 3:13; Lk. 21:34-36; Matt. 24:12; 2 Thess. 2:3-8).

35 | Triumphal Arch (2)

Futuristic Application

In the closing chapters of Revelation, we get a dramatic peep into a marvellous future. Before we look at that, we will sum up the traumatic past wich leads to that wonderful time ahead for the Christians.

Someone said, 'If there is one thing men learn from history, it is that men *never* learn from history!' There is something that Christianity doesn't learn from history. It is not to have divisions over non-essentials. One non-essential is whether the book of Revelation is in the past or in the future.

The book of Revelation opens by predicting the history of Christian witness. That is the first panel of seven lampstands, the triumphs and failures of the church. Then follow the usual visions explaining the meaning. These show that history is in the hands of Jesus, the Lamb of God, and that he triumphs.

The second panel of sevens—that of the seals—is the history of how the blood of the martyrs eventually won the Roman Empire to accept Christianity by the fourth century. The visions that follow show that the prayers and suffering of Christians were thus answered, but there are perils to come from other quarters.

The third panel is of seven trumpet warnings that the enemy Satan is advancing to attack the citadel of truth in a more subtle guise—that of false religions. The pagan priests who flooded into the churches were not really converted and brought in with them practices which originated from Babylon. The water of life was thus poisoned under the third trumpet and under the fourth trumpet, the light of truth was obscured; verse 12 says, 'darkened' These were the Dark Ages, an appropriate name.

Then under the fifth trumpet in the seventh century, comes the attack from the false prophet of the desert. The Saracen invasion wiped out the churches of North Africa during 150 years. The actual duration was foretold. But Satan outsteps himself for under the sixth trumpet the Turks break into south-east Europe in 1453. This causes the Reformation because the refugee monks brought the Bible to the West and, when translated, it became the open Bible of the Reformation, Revelation chapter 10.

The fourth and last panel showed how the bowls of anger are poured out upon unscriptural error. These purify the contaminated waters to bring life again— eternal life and also the sunlight of the gospel shines once again.

Under the sixth bowl, the Turkish Empire dries up from Europe and Palestine. It does so in the time scale accurately indicated, so that God's purposes are fulfilled in his Holy Land before the second coming of Christ.

Summation

So this marvellous insight demonstrates how that history is in the hands of the Lamb of God. He opens each page of traumatic history and he triumphs over Satan at each main stage. Finally, the kingdom of this world becomes the kingdom of God and of his Christ.

The final curtain rises on a new heaven and a new earth wherein dwells righteousness and joy and the redeemed radiate the irredescent light streaming from the Father and the Son.

All faithful believers will also triumph with him and sing, 'Salvation belongs to our God who sits upon the throne and unto the Lamb.... Worthy is the Lamb who has redeemed us out of every tribe and family and nation.... Hallelujah, the Lord God, the Almighty reigns'.

▼ CHECKPOINTS ▼

THE FUTURISTIC INTERPRETATION

Futuristic Application of panels 2 to 4 (Seals, Trumpets and Cauldrons)

Prophecy often fulfilled both ways (Matt. 17:10–13)
They are to be re-enacted literally during the Tribulation
(ie. during 7 years between Rapture and Judgement of nations)
Science of destruction has now made it possible
(ie. devastation through chemical, germal and nuclear warfare)
Appearance of anti-Christ, world government and multi-faith
Elijah comes literally (11:3,6). In John the Baptist it was spiritually

A Great Delusion

Satan deceives the whole world (Rev. 12:9; 19:20; 20:3,10)
Turning to myths in the last days (2 Tim. 4:4; 2 Thess. 2:9–11; 2 Pet. 3:3–7)
Well-known anthropologists admit no evidence of any stooping ape-men period
- 'Still to find evidence of very first bi-pedal apes' R.L. 1992 (yet he draws pictures of stooping ape-men)
- 'We have no fossils yet to tell us of the in between time' D.J. ('but we can picture it', he says)

- 'This fossil void is particularly frustrating' M.P. (but he assumes that it happened)
- Dubois 1880, hid leg bones of early man for 20 years (which proved upright walking)

Lessons from Revelation irrespective of interpretation

Glory of Jesus Unveiled
Inspires worship and Christian songs
We see the redeemed enjoying their Salvation
the Lamb controls history
Love story of the Bride and Christ concluded.

---

36 | How The Second Coming Will Affect You

Now that you have been thrilled by the insights into prophecy, you will want to know how it will happen.

First, I will describe how it will affect you by the main facts which all are agreed on. Then we will look at the other details which others are not so sure about. I find that often they can be clearly analysed from a humble and consistent examination of the Bible.

Your Seat on The Bench

What then is the clear factor which will make great changes to everybody's life? It is the statement that Jesus Christ will descend from heaven with great power and glory suddenly to judge the living and the dead. He will also judge the nations and everyone will have to give an account of his deeds.

So if you are saved, that is a wonderful tomorrow for you. In 1 Corinthians 6:2, 'Do you not know that the saints will judge the world and if the world will be judged by you, are you unworthy to judge even the smallest of matters.'

You may remark, 'But am I a saint? Do I qualify?' In the New Testament, the word 'saint' is used for a person who has accepted the free salvation of Christ.

So you see, a saint is a forgiven and cleansed sinner and as such, you will be with that triumphant host of saints and angels who descend from heaven to Jerusalem.

On Earth As It Is In Heaven

What is your answer to those who say to you, 'Why does God allow all this suffering, injustice and violence?'

I find the best answer is that one day soon the Lord is going to show the kind of earth he originally intended. That is after his return to reign.

The events after this are given in scripture but some are not sure about the order. That is not so important as the fact that they will happen. I believe, however, that a careful correlation of scriptures sorts out the following details:

Christ descends to judge the nations. (Matt. 25:31,32; Dan. 2:44 and 7:13)

The saved with their new bodies will descend with him (Rom. 9:19–23) and set up a just and happy rule upon earth of 1,000 years called The Millenium. This Millenium is described by nine writers in over twelve places in the Old and New Testament:

By Paul: 1 Corinthians 15:23–27 and Romans 8:19–23; by Daniel in chapter 7:13,14,27; by Isaiah in 2:1–5; 11:6–9; 65:17–25; by Ezekiel 48:35; by Joel 3:12–18; by Zechariah in chapter 14:16–21; and by John in Revelation 20:5,6.

Early Fathers Agree

All the early fathers of the first four centuries agree that the millenium follows Christ's coming. Papias, St John's disciple, says John taught it, and that the judgement of the unsaved will come at the end of the millenium (Rev. 20:5,11–15). Believers will not appear at this (Jn. 5:24,29).

Finally the universe will be cleaned up and the whole kingdom delivered up to the Father (1 Cor. 15:27,28; Rev. 21:27 to 22:5) and the Bible story ends with praise of joy and an invitation to you to be in that grand new world.

THE ORDER OF EVENTS TO COME

- **The Rapture.** Believers alive or dead will be caught up to meet Christ in the air, with changed bodies, (2 Thess. 2:1; 1 Thess. 4:17,17; 1 Cor. 15:51,54).
- **The Bride** (believers) married to the Saviour as in Matthew 25. The order then gives:
- **The Reward giving** (Matt. 25:14,30) called Christ's judgement or Bema (2 Cor. 5:10).
- **Descent of believers** with Christ to judge the nations (Matt. 25:31,32; Dan. 7:18; 1 Cor. 6:2).
- **Christ and the believers** will establish a happy just millenium (1 Cor. 15:23,27; Dan. 7:13,14,27; Isa. 2:1,5; Zech. 14:9–21; Rev. 20:5,6).
- **Millenium ends**. Unsaved dead raised for judgement (Jn. 5:29; Rev. 20:5,11–15).
- **Whole universe cleaned** up and delivered to the Father (1 Cor. 15:27,28; Rev. 21:1,5,6).
- **The eternal heavenly state** of purity, goodness and joy emanating from the Creator.

Conclusion

The universe began by being created good in Genesis chapter one, but sin and rebellion spoilt it. The creative Word, Jesus Christ redeemed it and us, so the Bible ends in Revelation with a new eternal heavenly state of joy and goodness which radiates with the divine source of all light.

Current events in Europe and the Middle East indicate that the return of the Lord draws near.

It is a privelege to know that we can belong to Christ to fulfill his purposes in our lives in these significant days.

Glossary of Terms

Age-day Theory   That Genesis days were an age or a great long period was held by the original founders of Creation Science.

Anthropic Principal   That the beginning of the Universe shows that man was its object, now held by a majority of scientists.

Assyriology   Archaeological research in Assyria (now North Iraq)

Astro physics   Study of physics and chemistry of heavenly bodies.

Big Bang Theory   That the universe had a beginning in an explosion of primary elements, as opposed to Steady State theory which thought there was no beginning.

Centresomes   A mechanism in the cell which draws each duplicate chromosome into the newly forming cell.

Chromosome   Each cell contains chromosomes which contain the instructions for making and sustaining an animal or plant. It is a double helical ribbon upon which instructions are recorded in code.

Cosmology   Science of the universe.

DNA   Short for Deoxyribonucleic Acid, the material of which genes and chromosomes are made.

Diploid   Both ends of an axis.

Genes   Are the smallest sections in the DNA instructions.

JEDP   Jehovah, Elokim, Deuteronomy, Priestly. Supposed sources from which it was conjectured that the Old Testament was compiled. Archaeology has since found that the ancients did not piece together literature in this way.

M RNA   Messenger Ribonucleic Acid. It is a copy of a section of DNA which the messenger takes to the ribosome production machines in the cell.

Meson   An unstable particle

Mitochondrion   The independent organelle in the cell which manufactures fuel to run the cell's machinery.

Neutron   A particle in an atom without a positive or negative charge.

Proton   A positively charged particle in an atom. How many these are determines the material's nature.

Quark   The basic building block of all atomic particles.

Ribosomes   The machines in the cell which decode the M RNA instructions and assemble protein chains of body parts as instructed.

Year-day prophecy   Certain prophecies use numbers in which days represent years as in Ezekiel 4:6

Now that you have read
WEIGHING THE EVIDENCE
Do you have a thirst for a more in depth
understanding? *Yes?*
Then why not enroll now for

EVIDENCE

FOR TRUTH

CORRESPONDENCE COURSE

◆ Three exciting illustrated volumes totalling 52
chapters, **Science, Archaeology** and **Prophecy** exploring
exciting historical discoveries, geological facts and
interpreting the amazing prophecies cited in the Bible.

◆ Discover the significance of contemporary events as
they inevitably lead up to Jesus Christ's second coming by
spending just a few hours per week.

◆ EVIDENCE FOR TRUTH is suitable for anyone of
secondary school age upwards. The course is bound to be
a very rewarding experience. Upon completion you
receive your own personalised certificate.

❑ **Easy ways to pay**
❑ **Learn in your own home**
❑ **Learn at your own pace**
❑ **Start at any time**

Course payment options: See order Form overleaf.

PTO

EVIDENCE
F O R   T R U T H

C O R R E S P O N D E N C E   C O U R S E

ORDER FORM

Please tick appropriate boxes

OPTION 1 *Any one set consisting of 1 study book and 1 workbook with tuition.*

❏ 4 monthly payments of £10 (£40 in total) **OR**
❏ A single payment of £39 for one set enclosed
       ❏ Science ❏ **or** Archaeology ❏ **or** Prophecy

OPTION 2 *The complete course in three sets consisting of 3 study books and 3 workbooks with tuition.*

❏ 12 monthly payments of £10 (£120 in total) **OR**
❏ A single payment of £115 for complete course enclosed
❏ I enclose my first month's payment of £10
❏ Send me details of Discounts for Church/Group use

Name Mr/Mrs/Miss_____

Address_____

_____

County_____

Post Code_____Tel:_____

Signature_____

PLEASE MAKE CHEQUES PAYABLE TO
EVIDENCE FOR TRUTH **AND SEND THIS FORM TO:**
Evidence For Truth, 13 Lismore Road, Eastbourne,
East Sussex BN21 3AY   Tel: (0323) 725231

Prices and details correct at the time of publication November 1993, however
publishers reserve the right to make alterations at their discretion.

▼ Please cut along this line ▼